BAJA'S GOLD

Treasure Along the Mission Trail

BAJA'S GOLD

Treasure Along the Mission Trail

Mill City Press

Mill City Press, Inc.
212 3rd Avenue North, Suite 570
Minneapolis, MN 55401
612.455.2294
www.millcitypublishing.com

ISBN - 1-934248-72-x
ISBN - 978-1-934248-72-0
LCCN - 2008935996

Typeset by James Arneson

Printed in the United States of America

Acknowledgements

$\mathcal{M}$any thanks to all who have helped with this book, first and foremost of course being Herman Hill himself. Herman has spent many hours relating the stories, correcting drafts as necessary, and adding details from his remarkable memory of events.

The many others who helped in one way or another are as follows:

Graham and Bonni Mackintosh – Graham is the author of four adventure books on the Baja, "Into A Desert Place", "Journey With a Baja Burro", "Nearer My Dog to Thee", and his latest, "Marooned – With Very Little Beer". Graham and Bonnie made many constructive suggestions, and I appreciate their contribution very much.

Jean Diaz, Cheryl Hill, Donna Martinson, and Pat and Fred Knirk also contributed valuable proofreading at various stages.

Thanks also to both Herman Hill and Prieta Diaz for loaning some of the photos that appear in the book.

Front cover picture courtesy of Mr. Wheelock – many thanks!

Introduction

I will never forget the first time I ever met Herman Hill. I was doing some volunteer work at the local health clinic operated by the Flying Samaritans, a crew of doctors who donate their time to the people of the village of Bahia de los Angeles. My job was to take blood pressure, pulse rate, and note the reason for the visit. People 70 or 80 would come in from the surrounding ranchos, most with better blood pressure readings than many people in their thirties!

A booming voice demanded "Whaddaya want to do, put that thing on my arm?" It was Herman Hill. His pulse rate and blood pressure were both better than my own. "And what is the reason for your visit, Mr. Hill?" "VIAGARA!" he announced loudly. He continued to explain as the non-English speaking patients listened with blank stares. "I don't use it for sex – it keeps me from peeing on my tennies! HAHAHAHAHAHA!!!!

At that point, one of the nurses appeared: "HERMAN! How are you?" Come over here sweetie!" He gave her a hug, and they disappeared into the clinic before I could tell him how long it would be before a doctor could see him. Herman seemed to know everyone, and everyone seemed to know him. He was in his mid-eighties, and still quite a ladies man. Many of his friends did not consider him 'safe' around any female from eighteen to eighty.

As time went on, I got to know Herman better, and loved to hear the tales of his life that he enjoyed sharing with everyone. They were really good stories. One day I asked him if he had written any of them down, and he said he had. He showed me three or four of what are now chapters in this book, none of which were more than a few paragraphs long. I borrowed one, expanded it to several pages, and returned it to him. He liked the changes, and agreed to sit down with me and dictate a book.

Over time, we settled into a routine that seemed to work. He would dictate a story into a tape recorder, I would listen, write up a list of questions, and he would answer them over one or two of his notoriously inebriating Margaritas, and if I was lucky, over a pot of his equally renowned seafood stews. I would then write up the chapter, and he would go over it and make changes. Chapter by chapter, the book got written.

I don't really know if I was able to do justice to his stories or not. The reader will have to make that judgment. All I know is they were great stories to hear around a fire at night. What I am most grateful for is that they did not go untold.

BAJA'S GOLD
Chapters

Growing Up in Las Vegas

CHAPTER 1

I was born in Los Angeles, California, and can still remember my earliest days there. The depression came along as the decade of the thirties began, and my family and I were caught in its grips as much or more than most families of modest income in the Los Angeles area.

Soon after the depression began, my father lost his job, and we were forced to live on welfare, "off the County" as we called it. It was a hard life for everyone then, but made easier for me by the fact that we had a strong family. My brothers and sisters all were very good to me. We stuck together, and helped out one another as best we could. My mother and father did what they could to make life bearable, in spite of the fact that we had almost no money. We were rarely hungry, as Mom always had a good nourishing dinner on the table at night, although meat dishes were very few and far between.

One day at dinner my father announced to us all that he was leaving for Las Vegas. He explained that his brother, my uncle, had arranged for him to join the railroad brakeman's union there, and there was a good chance he could get called for work on the railroad. This was a tremendous opportunity in those days, as unions were almost impossible to join. They were struggling to keep members who had been in the fold for years on the payroll. Newcomers who diluted the available jobs were not welcomed at all, but it seems my Uncle had the same gift for gab that my dad always had, and could talk his way into, or out of, just about anything. He had convinced the union local bosses to hire another man. It seemed an impossible task, but I guess all the boys in my father's family had the ability to lay on the "Blarney" pretty thick and smooth. Had anyone had the money to buy anything, my dad could probably have made it big as a salesman. But, they didn't, so he moved out of the house and went to live with his brother in Las Vegas.

After a few months, Dad had saved enough money to send for us. He sent Mom a big packet of train tickets for the whole family, and we left Los Angeles for our new life in the little railroad town called Las Vegas. I was sad to leave my friends behind, but looking forward to us all being together again, and having a father with a job! My father had done the best he could with the situation he had to work with, and managed to rent us a very small house near the railroad tracks on the edge of the town. It was part of a tract of railroad owned housing that had been built almost thirty years before. The railroad owned the houses, and would just deduct the rent from the employees pay. It was a slick setup. The Las Vegas of the early 1930's was a far cry from the neon studded metropolis of high rise hotels and gilded gambling palaces as we think of it today. It was a dusty desert town, dependent on the railroad junction it served. There were a few stores, wood frame houses, surrounding mines and ranches, and now it had us. I took to it immediately, loved the elementary school I entered, and immediately made a new circle of friends. It did not take long to forget my life of poverty in Los Angeles.

The house we lived in was just kitty-corner from what I learned was the infamous "Block 16" section of Las Vegas, what was then the red light district of town. From its earliest inceptions Las Vegas had its streak of vice, and even then had some legalized gambling. I was too young to really understand such things, but it did add a certain spice to the pulse of the town, one that I thoroughly enjoyed even at that tender age. The railroad junction in Las Vegas was one of the main links in the train routes between the East and West coasts. Its well deserved reputation as a wide open town made it a fun place to stop over on train trips to and from the Southern California coast.

We were much better off in Las Vegas than we had been in L.A. Dad was very good at endearing himself to the dispatchers, and got more assignments than most of the men who reported to the union hall every morning.

It didn't take my dad long to realize that being a conductor was a much better deal than being a brakeman. Using his usual persuasive techniques, he was able to talk himself out of the brakeman's tough and grimy job, and into the better life of a conductor. As a conductor, he made the same basic wage, but got a lot of tips to boot. It seemed the job was tailor made for a man with his personality. He was bright, cheerful, and could and did engage almost everyone in conversation. He got to know frequent riders on almost a personal basis, and the tips, especially from the Hollywood elite of those days, began to outpace his income from salary.

I was a little too young to really recognize the names and famous reputations of some of the people he met, but he brought some of them over to the house for supper on their stopovers, and I remember them to this day. The most famous of them was Will Rogers. He and Dad had a very similar sense of humor, and somewhat cynical take on the politics of the day, and they hit it off spectacularly. My mom was a great cook, and she would always pull out the stops for a celebrity visit, which all of us kids enjoyed as well. I was thrilled when Will Rogers showed great interest in some fossils I had found from my trips out into the surrounding desert. One night he even took out a coil of rope, and stood in the middle of our little living room showing us some rope tricks. He was really good at it, even after sharing several nips of Jack Daniels with my father. Mr. Rogers struck me as just a plain wonderful man, and I always looked forward to his visits. Unfortunately they became fewer as his fame mounted over time.

Another of my favorites was a guy named Pat O'Brien. Like Will Rogers, all the adults seemed to recognize him, and be very awed by his presence. Mr. O'Brien was very interested in investment, and he felt Las Vegas was going to grow a great deal in the future. He and my Dad were always talking about possible deals, but even though the family was doing much better by then, we really didn't have much money, not nearly enough for investments. He did buy up some property on the edge of town, and over the years it multiplied greatly in value. Mr. O'Brien had a good sense of humor too, and he even talked to me sometimes about the future. I remember him telling me "Herman, a boy your age has a fantastic opportunity in this town. Work hard, save your money, invest in property here and you will be a rich man some day." Well, I did manage the 'work hard' portion of his advice, but it all stopped there I am afraid! Around that time he and Bing Crosby started up the Del Mar racetrack just north of San Diego. My dad loved horse racing, and took me with him to the opening day there.

There were a lot of memorable characters in Las Vegas during those days. I wouldn't trade any other place, or any other time to grow up for the times I had in that wonderful place. Oh sure, it had its rough edges, its sub-rosa element, and a wild and woolly attitude that was perhaps a holdover from the only recently past days of the cowboy. That town had a lot of characters, and not only tolerated, but seemed to encourage them. Probably the most unique character of all was Death Valley Scotty. I remember him well. He was a very big man, with a red face. He always wore a flamboyant cowboy outfit with a colorful scarf, and promoted himself shamelessly in every way he could.

My dad told me that he had heard that Scotty had found some gold that had originally been mined by the Spanish. According to the story, some Indians ambushed the miners on their way out of the desert, killed them and stole their horses, but the Spanish had hidden the gold quickly and it got left behind. Many years later, Scotty had found the gold, still in saddlebags. Rather than just sell it and collect the money, he had come up with a grand scheme that one might expect from such a character. He claimed that he had made a great find, that there was infinitely more gold where he had found this, and that he, and only he, knew its location. It was perhaps my first lesson in how fascinated people can become with the idea of hidden gold, just awaiting the finding. In my subsequent life as a miner, I saw first hand this phenomenon many times. The lure of gold makes people do strange things. Anyway, as the story goes, he got all the newspaper headlines he was after, and became a well known figure from coast to coast. Spinning his tale of the gold mine, he went about his self-promoting and gathering of funds from a host of investors who were salivating at the thought of getting in on a good thing. He used money from these poor dopes when the original gold he had found ran out. He would buy more gold on the sly, and then claim it came from his mine.

One of the investors he found in the east became as interested in the phenomenal publicity that Scott was able to generate as the gold, and privately got him to admit the hoax. He agreed to bankroll Scotty, and to parlay his partnership into publicity for his businesses. Together, with the investor's money, they built a huge complex in the desert, which the press soon dubbed "Scotty's Castle." When the IRS moved in and wanted its share of the gold, Scott had to admit that there was no gold mine, and did so publicly. He lost most of his following then, but remained a character that was able to generate human interest stories the rest of his life.

I clearly remember one incident that involved Scotty. He liked to make a big splash at any public event, and never failed to enter parades that took place frequently in early Las Vegas. I attended one such parade as a child, and like the whole crowd, was excited when I saw Scotty coming down the center of Fremont Street sitting in the back seat of a big and shiny convertible. He was throwing out silver dollars to the crowd at random intervals. When he was abreast of where I was standing, he hurled one of the silver dollars in my direction. I will never forget what happened next. The coin struck a man standing close to me right in one eyepiece of his glasses. The glasses shattered, and the man went down like he had been hit over the head with a two by four. The dollar bounced away, and landed right at my feet! I grabbed it, not being able to believe my good luck. Some people in the crowd got the man to a sitting position, and I can still see the blood on his face from the broken glasses. I really didn't have too much time to feel sorry for him, I was too anxious to show my Dad the silver dollar I had gotten from Death Valley Scotty himself! I have always felt a little ashamed of that, and hope the guy wasn't hurt too bad. But, after all, I was just a kid, and hey, a buck is a buck!

My Introduction to Dynamite

*M*y lifelong search for gold had an early start. I was not even into my teens, and it was the height of the great depression in the United States. My uncle visited our house, and saw that my parents were hard-pressed to provide enough food to satisfy a growing boy. For many, there were no jobs, and no money, and little prospect for either in the foreseeable future. My Uncle understood immediately the situation in our household, and one night at dinner he said "Why don't I take Herman here off your hands for the summer, and teach him how to find gold? I am leaving for Death Valley tomorrow."

You can imagine my reaction. I liked my uncle very much, and the idea of spending the summer with the guys, and the prospect of finding gold, seemed like a dream come true to me. Taking responsibility for my upkeep was a truly generous gesture on my Uncle's part, and my parents, though hesitant, did not object. When I went to bed that night, my last thoughts were about going out with the guys, becoming a man, and finding gold. I could not wait for the morning to come.

In all the years since that night, I have wondered what my life might have been like had my uncle not made the offer, or had I not been enthusiastic in my acceptance. I imagine myself living an easy and safe life. I could have become an aircraft test pilot, an unexploded bomb dismantler, or Mohammed Ali's sparring partner. Any of these would have been tame compared to the one that fateful decision destined me to live, a life wandering the arid deserts of the Baja, where the dangers are many, and the comforts are few. The lure of that yellow metal is strong, and from that day forward, it has seeped in my soul, and will be there until the day I die. Of course, at the time I had no idea how fundamentally my life would be changed in the next few weeks. I just looked forward to an adventure in the goldfields.

We left for Death Valley the next morning. At my uncle's insistence I took only a small travel bag with a couple of changes of clothing, toothbrush, flashlight, and the very basics for life in the desert. He had all the tools needed to prospect, and I was to learn how to use them all. It is hard to relate how much I enjoyed those weeks with my uncle that summer of my life. I was big for my age, and was accepted as a near equal by the other men in the camp. For my part, I made sure I did my share of the work, pulled my own load, and was very keen to be seen as an asset rather than a liability. I loved the work during the day. It was hard, hot, and dirty work, but with moments of joy and satisfaction when the yellow began to show in the pan. I was solidly and incontrovertibly hooked for life. I loved the evenings around the fire, when the men would talk, and joke, while we ate supper. We took turns cooking the meals, and everyone was served from a big kettle. Every night it was some sort of concoction of inexpensive ingredients. It was always piping hot though, and after a full day of work, those were some of the most satisfying meals I have ever enjoyed. After supper there was time for smoking, some adult beverages, and more talk. The tales got taller as the night went on, but we all turned in fairly early as we were up with the dawn of each new day.

The theory we generally worked on was that gold, being heavier than the surrounding sand, had over the centuries worked its way down to the bedrock. You had to remove the overlay of sand and rocks, and dig down to the bedrock. The gold was concentrated in the little pockets directly above this hard impervious layer. And, indeed, it was my experience that it was there that the gold was found most often. So, our mining consisted of digging out round holes with steep sides, and hauling away the overlay of sand and rock until we got down to the hard bedrock layer. We would then begin to expand the walls of the pit, and follow the slope of the bedrock.

The main danger was that often if we had to go deep to stay on the bedrock level, the loose sand walls of the hole we were working in would suddenly, and without warning collapse. It had caused many a miner to lose his life, but fortunately for me, nobody died that way while I was there that summer. This constant danger made the work all the more tedious. No one wanted to take the time and effort to shore up the walls.

After a couple of weeks of work, my uncle and I had a canvas pouch of gold that was growing heavier each day. It was not much really, for all the hard work we put in to get it, but this was the depression, and if you had anything at all, it was a lot. One night, the talk turned, as it often did, to how we could find more gold. One old timer said that he felt that there was probably another layer of gold dust UNDER the bedrock, which was only a few feet thick where we had been working. This theory sparked a lively debate that went on for several evenings, until one night, some one suggested, "Well, why don't we get some dynamite and find out?"

There was only one flaw with the plan. Dynamite cost money, and we had precious little of that. After polling the group, we came up with four men who would each chip in the ten cents it cost for a single stick of dynamite. The next day, somebody drove into the nearest town and came back with four sticks of the stuff, wrapped in shiny red paper. There was a long coil of fuse and blasting cap for each stick.

The talk that night around the fire was a careful analysis of how our investment in the explosives should be put to work. One of the holes we had worked that looked about right was selected. It was decided that all four sticks of dynamite would be used at once, in a square pattern, so that we would be sure to remove a sizeable chunk of the bedrock and could at last find out what was under it. It seemed like a good plan to me. They discussed details such as how deep to drill the holes, how long to make the fuses, and finally, who should light them off. I was listening intently to the planning, when I realized they were all looking at me.

"You know," said one, "that Herman there has done a hell of a job since he has been here. I think he could do it." They all nodded and there was a general consensus that I was the ideal candidate for the job.

"You are young and agile kid, and light on your feet. Whaddaya think?"

I looked at my uncle, expecting some objection, but he was intently studying his coffee, and said nothing in my behalf.

"Sure, I can do it!" I heard myself saying.

Inside I was scared as hell, but I wanted so much to be accepted by these men, and at my tender young age, was convinced that the honor they were bestowing on me was due to my excellent qualifications, and that I had earned their respect at last.

That is how I found myself the next morning down in a hole with a box of matches and four sticks of dynamite that looked as big as telephone poles to me. Everything was set. The holes had been drilled, and I had been carefully briefed as to exactly what to do, and in what order. They told me to put one stick of dynamite in each of the four holes, making sure the blasting caps that went between the fuse and the stick were firmly in place. I was to put each stick in its hole, lay out the fuses carefully so they didn't cross each other, light them, and then quickly climb the ladder out of the hole and join the rest of the group. The fuses were extra long, and they assured me I would have ample time to complete these tasks and be far away when the dynamite blew. Then they all left me in the pit with the dynamite and gathered on a knoll several hundred feet away to watch, and wait.

I was alone in the hole. It was the most lonely I have ever been in my life. I wanted desperately to climb up the ladder and run after them, yelling "Hey, thanks for giving me this honor, but I really don't feel worthy of it." But, I knew to do that would have disgraced me in the eyes of all of the men I looked up to so much, and was unthinkable.

So, I put the sticks of dynamite into the holes, lowering them by the fuses until I felt them hit bottom. I then separated the fuses so there was no overlap, and one by one, I lit them. I was not at all prepared for the violence with which the fuses burned. It was shocking to me, not only did they sputter and spit sparks loudly, but each released a cloud of pungent and acrid bluish smoke. By the time I got the fourth one lit, the small cramped hole had filled with smoke. I had trouble seeing, and was coughing so hard that it was difficult to catch my breath, but I could see the flame of all four fuses, and it was time to get the hell out of that hole. I could barely see the ladder, but found it and started up. I guess the adrenalin was really pumping, and I hit that rickety ladder running in a desperate need to get to the top. At about the third or fourth step up, my foot dislodged the ladder step, and I fell to the bottom, my legs shearing off all the rungs underneath me. The ladder and I hit the bedrock floor together in a pile.

The four fuses continued their fitful sparking, and the smoke was becoming unbearable. I lay there on my stomach for an instant that seemed like an hour, trying to assess my situation and figure out what to do, whatever it would take to survive. As the guys had promised, the fuses were long, and there was still a couple of feet of fuse leading to each of the holes. I did not know if I could put out all four of the fuses successfully in the time I had or not, so I decided on another approach. One by one, I grabbed each fuse, put my foot partially over the hole, and jerked the fuse, blasting cap and all, out of the dynamite. One by one I yanked the fuses free, and tossed them aside. Now the dynamite could not explode. I took my shirt off and put it over my head to try to keep the gasses and smoke from choking me, but it was only partially successful. I lay there for a moment, listening to the popping and sizzling of the fuses, when a sickening thought struck me. The blasting caps! I knew each contained a powerful charge of fulminate of mercury, designed to shock the dynamite into explosion. They were still attached to the fuses, and if they went off, in that enclosed space, I was facing a concussion that could cost a lifelong loss of hearing, or much, much worse – especially four of them. My life was still very much in danger. I ripped the shirt off of my head, and began scrambling around the floor of the pit looking for the lighted fuses. I saw one, grabbed it just behind the lit end, and ran my hand down the other direction until I felt the blasting cap. I snatched it off, and began looking for the second one. I found it, and the third one, and rendered each harmless, removing the cap and stamping on the fuse until it was extinguished, or looked extinguished. The fourth one gave me trouble. I could hear it, but I could not see it. The hole was so full of smoke now that I could not see a thing; it was extremely painful to even open my eyes. My only chance was to find it by hearing. It was hard to hear anything over the hammering of my own heart, and once again, I had to force myself to be calm, and act with disciplined control in my search for the remaining fuse. Slowly, on all fours, I moved toward where I thought the sound was coming from, but could see nothing. It had been quite a while by now since I had lit the fuses, and I was really getting worried. I gave up on the direction I had been going, and struck out on a new course across the rocky floor, on my hands and knees. The walls of the excavation made sounds reverberate, and it was very difficult to get a bearing. It sounded to me like I was going in the wrong direction, so I turned around, and immediately saw a flickering on the far side of the hole. The fuse and blasting cap lay behind part of the broken ladder. I scrambled over to it, now in near panic, and groped for the fuse. There was no choice but to grab for the lit end, which was all I could see in the blackness of the hole. I slightly burned myself, but at that point, a burn was pretty low on the list of things that could happen to me. I whisked my hand down the fuse, felt the blasting cap on the end, and flung it loose. I didn't bother to try putting out the rest of the fuse, because it was less than a foot in length! In a few seconds it burned out, and there was silence in my own little private hell. All I could hear was my own breathing, and the pounding of my heart. I put my shirt over my head again to try to keep out some of the smoke, and between coughs, yelled at the top of my lungs. But, my buddies were safely ensconced on a knoll a safe distance away, and could not hear me. I am sure most of them were thinking, "I wonder what is happening, it should have gone off by now." And maybe a few were even thinking, "I wonder where Herman is?

Nobody came. I lay on the floor of the hole and choked back the nauseous fumes, and slowly the smoke dissipated. Still nobody.

Finally, I screamed bloody murder, "Goddam it, come and help me!"

At length, a coil of rope hit the floor next to me. Even now, nobody wanted to come close to the mouth of the hole until they knew for sure what happened to the dynamite. I pulled on the rope, and it went taught, so I pulled myself out of my would-be grave, and once more drunk in the sweet, clear, clean, desert air.

I was sick for two days. My lungs ached, I had a headache and a stomach ache, and I felt miserable. The fumes I had inhaled had taken their toll. But, I felt at the very least I had earned the respect of the miners. I learned differently when about two days later, the discussion turned to the dynamite that was left in the holes we had drilled.

One of the miners had the nerve to say "Herman, you really did a good job there kid, why don't you go down and fish them things out so we can use them again?" But I had learned a lot about smoke during the whole fiasco. And the most important of all, is that I learned not to let anyone blow smoke up my ass. It is one I still heed to this day.

"Why don't you do it? I asked. "I am just a kid, that's man's work!"

Cora

$\mathcal{T}$ he house my father chose for our family in Las Vegas was almost directly across the railroad tracks from the town's infamous red light district. Everyone referred to it as "Block 16," and the action there was typical of the wild, spontaneous, unpredictable and fun-loving city that was Las Vegas in the 1930s. Prohibition had been repealed, and prostitution, while technically not legal, was "winked at" among most residents, and ignored or enjoyed by the others. In those days, even more than today, it was a town with a wide-open throttle.

I was a young boy at the time, and didn't really know much about prostitution, or most things of a sexual nature. All I knew was that my father, although he never mentioned it around the house, was in favor of it, and may have even partaken of it on occasion. My mother thought it was scandalous.

My lifetime platonic love affair with Cora started innocently enough: One day I crossed the tracks following my usual shortcut to town. A young woman sat watching me from the back porch of a cottage in one of the Block 16 wooden buildings. As I passed by, she called, "Hey, you're Herman Hill, aren't you?"

"Yes ma'am." I was a little surprised she knew me, because I didn't recall ever seeing her before.

"I heard what you did for Mrs. Graham the other day. I think that was real nice of you, Herman."

I'd been passing Mrs. Graham's house one day the week before, when she offered me a nickel if I would go into town and pick up her groceries. Mrs. Graham was pretty old, lived alone, and she didn't walk too well, so I could see why she didn't want to go herself. I lugged two heavy bags from the store to her house.

Later that night at the supper table I told my family about earning five cents that day. My father questioned me, and when he found out how I'd earned that nickel, he surprised me by disapproving. "Herman, Mrs. Graham can't really afford that, you know. It was not right for you to take money from her for what you did. You should have done it as a favor, because it was the right thing to do, not for what little money she might have." I hadn't really thought about it that way, and began to feel ashamed of what I had done. My father realized how I felt, and went on to say, "Herman, you have your whole life ahead of you. You will make a lot of money in your lifetime. Mrs. Graham won't be able to earn much more money the rest of her life. She needs it more than you do. What do you think, son? Wouldn't it be doing the right thing to go give the nickel back tomorrow?"

"I will Dad, I promise."

And so, I gave back the five cents, and really felt good about it. I wound up getting her stuff from town pretty regularly, and even looked forward to doing my good deed. And this young woman sitting on the porch had found out about it.

"Oh, yeah," I stammered. "Well, I figured it was the right thing to do," I said, quoting Dad. I'd moved closer to her, and I could see her beautiful blue eyes, perfect complexion, and shoulder-length black hair, which seemed to shine. I can still smell the perfume she was wearing. I got very nervous, and felt strangely attracted, yet at the same time a little uncomfortable.

"Where are you headed now, Herman?" she asked. "Goin' into town?" I nodded. "Wait just a minute", she said, and disappeared briefly into the cottage. She came out holding two empty Coca Cola bottles. "Here's a nickel Herman, go trade these for two full ones and we'll have a cold coke, ok?"

I brought back the two cokes that day, and we sat on the back steps of her cabin and talked. I found out her name was Cora, and that she was from Los Angeles. She seemed to have a slightly southern accent, and I asked her about it. "Oh, yeah," she laughed, "Well I was born in the south, but I have lived in L.A. for years now and pretty well lost it. But, around here some folks seem to like a southern accent. They think it's cute or something. So I guess I'm sort of getting it back!"

"What do you do here?" I asked innocently. She looked at me and smiled, "Oh I just help out Mama."

I knew who Mama was. I had seen her around town before. Years later I understood that she was the Madam, but in those days, I just saw her as the boss. She was a very pleasant looking older black lady who had put on a few extra pounds over the years. Almost everyone in town knew Mama, and most liked her. She carried herself with dignity, and ran a no nonsense house. She had a reputation of being strict but fair with employees and customers alike. Hers was a clean establishment, in which rules were followed or else. To feel the full wrath of Mama's anger was indeed a fearsome thing. She demanded standards of her girls, but protected them like a mother hen if they were in any way mistreated. Likewise she greeted her customers with enthusiasm and good humor, but brooked no infraction of standards of acceptable behavior, and applied quick and appropriate reprisal to anyone foolish enough to break them. Her husband was a tall slender guy with a walrus mustache, and a funny accent. I think he was Dutch or something similar. He didn't talk much. He left that to Mama. She worked the front of the house, dealing with people, and he ran the back, overseeing the bar, ordering supplies, and paying off the police. The cops kept an eye on block sixteen, and any problems were handled quietly, quickly, and informally, so the place never made the newspapers.

We talked while we drank the coke. She asked me a lot of questions, and seemed genuinely interested in my answers. When I left, she said "We'll have to do this again some time Herman, OK?" Wow, it sure was ok with me! She was way too young to have been my mother, but I was certain she would make somebody a good one. She was so pretty, and nice, and really seemed to care about me. I began looking for her as I took my shortcut into town, and if she was there on her back step, almost always we would go through our familiar routine, me bringing back the cokes, and us sitting there, talking, and drinking them.

She never mentioned her family at all, I really don't know if she still had one or not. She said many times that she hoped someday to live in San Francisco. She had been there once when she was about my age, and had found it an exciting and interesting place. As we spent more time together, I opened up to her too, and told her some things I wouldn't ever have been able to say to my own mother or father. She was always understanding, and never seemed bored or disinterested in what I had to say. We talked as I had never talked to any adult before, and about any subject you could think of. I fell deeply in puppy love with Cora, with her clear blue eyes, beautiful white teeth and smile. She was quick to laugh, a sound I would remember all my life.

Every once in a while we would be interrupted. A voice from inside, usually Mama's, would call "Cora? Cora honey, you have a gentleman caller to see you." Cora would crush out her cigarette, finish the coke, and apologize for having to go. I guessed innocently that she was so nice she had a lot of friends like me coming over to see her. Every month she would take a vacation for a few days. She said Mama had a place where she and the other girls stayed in Los Angeles, and she used to go shopping and to the doctor to have checkups. That kind of bothered me, because I didn't want her to have anything wrong with her, she was so young.

I remember one time we were talking about things that had happened around town. I told her that my Mom had said not to go over to the Brooks' house any more. Old man Brooks had gone to jail for some reason, and Mom didn't want me associating with the family any more. I had known Billy Brooks slightly, but we weren't really friends. He was one grade behind me in school. I told Cora about it, and I can remember her saying "Well, Herman, you might want to think about that. I mean, you should do what your mother tells you, but you should really think about Billy a little more. Do you think it is any fault of his that his Dad went to jail?" No, I hadn't thought of that at all. She was right though, I can remember thinking even then. "Even his Dad," Cora continued, "Maybe he did something wrong, but maybe it was because he loved his family and wanted to provide a good life for them. Maybe he didn't want to do what he did, but he felt he had to. You will learn Herman, that sometimes folks have a way of judging people because of what happens to them, and they don't stop to think how or why it happened. They just judge them, and look down on them. They just...." I waited for her to continue, but she paused. When I looked up at her, sitting on the steps to her room, I saw that there were tears on her beautiful cheeks. She took out a Kleenex and wiped them away. I couldn't figure out then why she had gotten so emotional about Billy's dad getting thrown in jail. I didn't understand her tears then, but I did later, and have all my life tried hard not to judge people, lest I be judged by them.

I can't really remember how long we went on with our back porch conversations, but it was several months at least. One day I went by, and she was not there. A couple of cottages down, Mama's husband and another guy were busy cleaning up a mess on the back steps. It looked like blood to me. When he saw me, the man in the walrus mustache and foreign accent yelled at me "You kid. You go get out now. GO!" I did as he said. The very next day, workmen were busy putting up a very tall fence around the back of the cottages. There was a driveway behind the building where customers could gain access to the place with discretion. They fenced off the whole block in back, and I had to change my shortcut into town. After that I saw Cora every once in a while, but we could only wave at each other, and I never got to talk to her again. Mama's girls weren't allowed on the streets either.

I only heard from her one more time. In our conversations once I had told her I wanted to start saving money for a wristwatch, something almost no boys my age had in those days. A few weeks later, a guy who worked at Mamas doing odd jobs saw me on the street in town. "Hey Herman, I have something for you from Cora." It was a beautiful gold plated watch with a real leather band. Of all the gold I have ever possessed, I valued, and will continue to value, that the most.

I wore the watch for years until it broke. I couldn't bear parting with it, so I put it in a drawer for many more years, until in all my moves, I finally lost track of it. The watch is gone, but not my memories of beautiful Cora. I have remembered her, and in some ways loved her, all my life. Many times, staring into my campfire coals in the evening, I have wondered what happened to her, and if she ever got to live that wonderful life in San Francisco she dreamed so much about. I hope she did. More than once I have seen her smiling face again in my dreams. To me she is still a beautiful girl barely into her 20's. God bless you Cora, wherever you are.

My Beloved Las Vegas

CHAPTER 4

Las Vegas shares a lot of physical and historical qualities with the Baja; maybe that is why I love them both. The two are remote, have Spanish origins, and are centered on that life-giving substance, water.

In prehistoric times, the area was much wetter than it is today. It was made up of marshlands with abundant water, and vegetation of types not found there today. As time passed, the weather changed. The waters evaporated or retreated underground to be trapped within the porous earth upon which the city is situated today. Recently bones were found of mammoths no more than 10,000 years old, showing how recently the change took place.

Las Vegas was extremely remote, and not located along or near any substantial trails in the early days. Being surrounded by hundreds of miles of parched and forbidding desert, it was known only to the Native Americans until quite recently. In 1829 a Mexican trader by the name of Antonio Armijo was leading a sixty man contingent south on the trail to Los Angeles. One of Armijo's best scouts, Rafael Rivera, was sent to see if he could find any source of water in the region to the southwest of the established trail. At that time, the vicinity was all unexplored territory. Rivera could not believe what he saw at the spot which would become known as Las Vegas. There were several abundantly flowing artesian wells, and a rich year-round supply of fresh, sweet water. Rivera hurried back to the 60 man main party, and they diverted their path. From then on, almost all travel between the great salt lakes and Los Angeles went through what was known as Vegas. This shortened the original route significantly, and providing a respite with unlimited water supplies. Over the years maps began adding the "Las" to the name Vegas, which means "The Meadows" in Spanish.

Fourteen years later, John C. Fremont camped at the springs, having no idea the streets, buildings and schools that would one day bear his name. The Mormons became interested in the springs because of their proximity to the settlements in Utah. They sent a detachment of troops and settlers there in the mid 1850's, built an adobe fort, part of which still stands on Las Vegas Boulevard. The Mormons for a time had a successful settlement there with farming and mining projects underway, but were driven out by continual hostile Indian raids.

Nevada became a state during the Civil war. It is still known as the "Battle Born State." After statehood was granted, things happened at a more rapid rate. Within 40 years, the Indian uprisings in the area were quelled, and the first railroad was built into the growing little settlement. Las Vegas became a vital link in the "San Pedro, Los Angeles, and Salt Lake Railroad." The very first terminal was built at the spot where the "Plaza" hotel stands today. The modern terminal is still there, and the hotel was built over it, quite an undertaking for the time. It remains the only railroad station in the world located within the walls of a casino. Only in Las Vegas! The railroad was bought up by the huge Union Pacific Company, which began running more frequent freight and passenger service through the town. From an original shanty town of tents, the city grew with new and modern wooden buildings. Most of the growth was along Fremont Street which was unpaved and extended out from the terminal.

About the time my family moved to Las Vegas, two things happened to greatly enhance the fortunes of the growing city. First, gambling, which had been outlawed in 1910, but had then only gone underground and made the policemen rich, was again made legal in Nevada. That same year, construction began on the Hoover Dam, only 30 miles from Las Vegas on the Colorado River. That project soon employed over 5,000 construction workers, and went a great distance toward sheltering Las Vegas from the full terrible impact of the great depression.

Being from a relatively poor family, Las Vegas provided me the opportunity that few other cities of the time could have. My childhood and teenage years were very happy ones. By the time I graduated from high school, the depression was on its way out, but several of the projects put into place by Franklin Roosevelt were still in place. When I graduated from high school, I went to work for the Civilian Conservation Corps, and earned some pretty good money for a guy my age. I loved the work, and remember that I used to put in extra hours on my off time helping unload ore trucks from the surrounding mines. Even in those days, I had a keen interest in mining. By the time I left the CCC, I had saved up what I considered to be quite a bit of money. Mr. O'Brien had told me years before to buy land, and now I had the money, so I went out looking. I found a 40 acre plot a couple of miles out of town on Fremont Street. At that time it was still unpaved, and considered a remote spot. The guy wanted a dollar an acre and I decided to buy it. When I told my dad however, he strongly discouraged me, saying it was so far out in the desert it wasn't worth more than twenty five cents an acre, and I would be wasting my money. So, instead I bought a 1932 Ford coupe, which greatly impressed the girls, but didn't do a lot for my future. Today, I do not want to even think what that land, now on what is known as 'the strip', and covered with multi-million dollar casinos, would be worth. On the other hand, the memory of the company of cute gals that deuce coupe brought me is worth a lot too.

I Find My Paradise in Baja

*M*y lifelong interest in prospecting, even at a young age, predetermined that I would go into the business in some capacity or another. I loved the lure of finding and working with precious metals, and that part of the profession I have never ceased to love and want to be a part of every day of my life. There is another aspect however, that slowly grew in the background, without my noticing very much at first.

As time went on, the whole phenomenon of normal life began to overtake me, one step at a time. I met a woman I thought I loved, got married, and added links to my chains every day. First link – marriage, then rent on a nicer house, car payments, insurance payments, utilities. Before I even realized it, I had taken on the entire catastrophe of normal life. I felt growing pressures to conform to the confining restrictions of society's expectations. I began to realize more clearly than ever that these were not really only expectations – they were demands!

To be a good husband, and some day soon a father, I was expected to get a good job, do well, rise within an organization, and provide for my family. It was obvious to me at that point that I could no longer consider work to be a manifestation of interests, enthusiasm, and following my own calling. It would have to be make money –

now – in the future, and at a steady, predictable rate to match all my payments.

Prospecting does not lend itself to such steady incremental accrual of money. It is much more feast and famine. The feasts would be fine for everyone, but the famine would label me as selfish, undependable, and a failure at providing for my family, as was my obligation as seen through the eyes of society.

So, under this pressure, I bent. I bent to the sacred dictates of whatever God rules the sanctity of "Providing for One's Family." I actually went to work for someone else! And, I hated it! I was still working with metals, which I loved, but I was paid for the time I spent, rather than my luck, skill, and accumulated knowledge as I preferred. I had a steady job with a steady income, and everyone was happy. My wife was happy. Her family was happy. My family was happy. My neighbors saw me as a stand-up sort of family guy. My boss was happy. The only one unhappy by the whole setup was me.

I went through a period of abject unhappiness until I had the opportunity to start my own small foundry business, which was much more my style. At last I could work hard, work long, work smart, and my income depended on my own motivation and skill. I liked that a lot better than trading time, part of my life, for money. At first my business, small though it was, did very well. As it grew, so did its complexity. There was more of an income, but also more of a need for cash flow, adherence to rules, regulations and tax laws. The amount of red tape involved in having employees overwhelmed me, and I found myself working more with paper than with metal.

I was beginning to learn more and more about myself as I went through life. That I was not cut out to work for an hourly wage was a given. Even having my own business removed me from what I loved to do the most. I loved prospecting, being by myself in the desert, and waiting for, and hoping for, the big strike. The chance of finding a big nugget motivated me far more than the lure of a weekly paycheck.

Nor was I cut out by nature to be a good husband. My wife, as any wife would, had the annoying desire to have me around the house on a regular basis, which did not fit well with my need to wander the desert for weeks at a time. I felt sort of like the man who buys an expensive pair of shoes. Everyone compliments him, and tells him how good they look. What they don't know is that they don't really fit right, and begin to rub, and then to cause blisters. Such was my life, until some one offered me a comfortable pair of sandals!

A fellow who had worked for me for a while came to see me, and brought with him exciting news. He had just returned from Mexico, where he had been working for another American in a gold mining and milling operation based at Hermosillo, in the Mexican state of Sonora. This American was looking for someone with experience in prospecting, and was open to a percentage deal. The idea of such a change in lifestyle was enhanced by the fact that I liked my ex-employee. He had been an honest man, and a hard and intelligent worker, and I trusted him. He spoke highly of the Gringo he was now working for in Hermosillo, which also encouraged me. Within a week, we were on our way to Sonora.

After I had been in Sonora for a couple of days, had met my new boss, and had fallen in love with Sonora as I had with Nevada, I knew what I had to do. I cannot explain the joy that I felt at the idea of once more being free to roam the desert, look for gold and silver, and not worry about paying the phone bill. There was no phone in my new home. I liked the owner of the operation, and we seemed to click on the idea of what was to be done, and how. We struck an agreement quickly, and I headed back to Las Vegas. On the long drive home, I dreaded the necessity of having to share my plans with my wife, as she was no longer included in them.

As it turned out, I did not need to worry about breaking the news to her. She was more interested in keeping the house than she was in keeping me, I soon discovered. I am not sure which of us looked forward to the radical change in lifestyle the most, but both did so with obvious relief and enthusiasm. I took a very dim view of the idea of being a husband, and she had an equally dim view of my ability to do so to her requirements. Within another week, I was headed south again for a lifetime of adventures, all my worldly possessions fitted neatly in the trunk and back seat of my ancient car. I was driving the old car, as my wife had kept the new one.

My spirits rose to old heights as I adjusted to my new life in Sonora. I was back in the desert, and seeking gold and silver again, as I had in the happiest days of my life. Few people ever have the chance to go back in time, but I felt I had. I was doing what I had been doing years ago, and it seemed that the whole world had gone back with me!

The life in Mexico was much like what Las Vegas had been for me in the beginning. There were few laws, rules, and restrictions, and the desert was wild, wide open, and had yet to become subject to society's creeping tentacles of regimentation, bureaucracies and the curtailment of personal initiative as it had in Nevada. I was one of the rare people whom fate had given a second chance in life, and I was determined not to sway again from my god-given abilities, my need for independence, and my enjoyment of solitude in the desert. In this, I have been successful.

I was once again back in my element, loving every day of my life, and felt the pressures and obligations of Nevada shedding from me as the desert animals shed hair with the coming of summer. It is likely I could have stayed in Sonora permanently, but fate had other plans for me. After only a year and a half in my new life, another opportunity presented itself, and once again, I chose to gamble on the unknown, rather than stand pat with the hand I had been dealt.

A fellow I met talked with soaring enthusiasm about an even more remote place than Sonora. According to him, it was a prospector's paradise – untamed, wild, bereft of life's most rudimentary pleasures, but with a stark beauty and vast store of unfound gold and silver. Needless to say these things intrigued me, but the rest of the opportunity he described sealed the deal for good. It seemed there was a very rich find near the town of La Paz, on the Baja peninsula, that was waiting for some one to come and exploit it. As the story went, a friend of his had been working a very lucrative seam, but had fallen ill, and had to return to the States. He had covered over the claim, and wanted to sell it to some one who would work it, and send him a percentage of the profits.

As is usually the case with me, my heart prevailed over my head, and I made the decision to go once again. I was leaving a situation that was ideal for me, one I loved and had prospered in, and leaping headlong into another that I knew not of. It was a very foolish thing to do, fraught with all kinds of pitfalls and possible disappointments. But, it involved gold, the desert, and the chances for riches, which made it right for me. Within another month, I was driving my car off the ferry at La Paz, and soon I first set foot on my beloved Baja California.

In my new setup, I had a partner, which I usually do not prefer, but he was an affable fellow, honest, hard-working, and a good companion around the campfire, and we got along quite well. We found the mine, began working it, and soon were taking out nuggets of excellent size and quality. Normally I do not like hard-rock mining. I am much more at home with placer gold, or silver. But, it makes sense to go where the gold is, and this was a very productive seam of quartz. We had no idea of what we would find as we followed it deeper into the mountain. It could just peter out, or end abruptly. It could go on and on, deeper and deeper, until it got too dangerous to follow, and would require a bigger operation than the two of us. Or, and we both knew it, it could suddenly and without warning provide us with a giant nugget measured in kilos instead of grams. It had happened in the Baja before.

For once in my life, I had begun to save up money. Even my trips to the gaming tables at Las Vegas, which I allowed myself every few months, could not completely diminish my monetary reserves. In fact, on more than one occasion, they actually added to it! Things went well for another couple of years, until my partner began to lose energy. He just didn't appear well to me. This went on for some time, until I prevailed upon him to go to the doctor in La Paz. He finally agreed, and returned with the news that he had been told he was very ill, and needed to return to the states for treatment. We didn't see it as a great problem at the time. We decided that he would go for his treatment, and in the meantime I would continue to work the claim and guard our things until he returned. What we did not know is that he was never to return.

After he had been gone for about six weeks, I received a letter from him. I was astonished to read that his diagnosis had been Arsenic poisoning! Unbeknown to either of us, there was a very high arsenic level in the rock we had been working, and it was slowly being accumulated in our bodies. I too was in great danger, although I had yet to show any signs of the poisoning. He suggested that I sell the claim to a larger outfit that would have the proper equipment to mine the seam. Since it had been a good producer, I had no trouble finding a buyer. He told me to keep half of what I got for the claim, and send him half. But, it had been his in the first place, and I had made plenty from it, much of which I still had, so I just sent him the whole thing. I never saw him again, but I heard that he recovered and lived for several more years. I decided to head north.

I have always been a voracious reader, and I had read much about the Jesuits and their century-long stay in the Baja. The most intriguing thing to me was the persistent mention of gold. Rumor had it that the holy fathers had a real knack for coming up with gold and silver, and were not above using their Indians to procure it for them. I felt very lucky I had not been as susceptible as my partner to the buildup of arsenic and that I had better not press my luck. I wanted to give up hard rock mining. I had a good amount of money saved up from working the claim, and no reason to hang around La Paz any longer. But mostly, I was ready to go and find out what I could about the Jesuits and their gold that I had heard and read about. I talked to everyone I met that had any knowledge of the mission days, and pored over maps of the central Baja. Once again I was heading out into the unknown, this time in a new pickup truck I had bought on my last trip to Las Vegas. I had drawn a big circle around my destination – a remote mission at San Borja.

The Mystery Unfolds -
My First Clue

CHAPTER 6

$\mathcal{T}$he sound of an airplane engine awoke me from a sound sleep. I glanced at my watch. It was two o'clock in the morning. The full moon gave a silvery glow to the desert around me, the hills and canyons, making them seem almost eerily like a snow covered scene from an arctic land. I was camped on a high ridge, and the noise from the plane echoed off the canyon walls below me. Although it flew without running lights, I could see it clearly in the moonlight, approaching from the south directly down the canyon center. As it got almost abreast of me and slightly below, the pilot pulled back on the throttle. The Lycoming engine on the Piper Cub slowed and sputtered. I saw a large object drop from the plane, and watched it fall to the floor of the canyon. The engine roared back to full throttle, the plane climbed, banked, and made a 180 degree turn back to the south, and was soon gone from sight and hearing.

It was clear to me what was happening. Arising immediately I began to break camp. The moonlight enabled me to gather everything up without using a light. As I prepared to leave, I saw the expected, a pair of headlights approaching on the dirt road that ran along the valley floor. It was a classic drug drop, and I had seen many of them in my time in the mountains. Any veteran Baja traveler knows that it is best to keep a good distance between themselves and the drug runners. They do not like witnesses, and would not think twice about eliminating anyone who stumbled onto their clandestine activities. Any resulting corpses would likely not be discovered for months, if ever, in these remote reaches of the desert. So, I deemed it prudent to leave immediately, and head deeper into the mountains, away from any roads until they had finished their criminal business below.

About seven the next morning, I reached a spot that looked promising and set up camp again. I spent the rest of the day prospecting the area with disappointing results. Returning to my camp that afternoon, I set about making a dinner of beans, tortillas, and some canned meat. It was very simple food, typical camp fare that didn't require much preparation time, but it was good, and filling, and I had grown to like and look forward to such meals. After eating, I poured myself a sizeable glass of tequila, as was my habit in the evenings, and watched the sun go down. I was treated to one of those very special Baja sunsets of hues of red and purple and vermillion, God's light show for which there is no cost of admission. The sky darkened and the colors faded. I kept the fire going, not so much for the heat, as it was not very chilly, but more for the cheery feeling it afforded. This was not the place I had intended to prospect. I was sure the drug runners had left by now, and I resolved to go back to my original camp the following day.

I was on my second tequila, and the sky had darkened further, when I noticed something on the hill adjacent to my camp that reflected the light of my fire. "Strange," I thought to myself. I was way too far out of civilization for it to be a discarded bottle or can. What could be reflecting the light so brightly? It piqued my curiosity, and I vowed I would go see what it was with the next morning's light.

When I went to look the next morning however, I could find nothing. There was no bit of glass or metal that could have reflected the light of my fire. I carefully searched the area from which the reflection came, but still found nothing. I decided to keep the same camp for one more night. The prospecting here was little more than ordinary, and I found only a few samples worthy of keeping that day. What kept me there was the curiosity as to what could have been making the reflection from my campfire. That night as soon as it was dark I built another fire. There it was again, a strong bright reflection. This time I didn't wait until morning, but went out with a flashlight, determined to pinpoint the light source. What I finally found didn't make sense to me at first. It was a black, highly polished rock wedged into the side of a sheer hillside rise. I examined it carefully, and discovered that it had been ground to a perfect flatness. Straight across its middle was a single graven horizontal line. It had obviously been worked by human hands. I decided to investigate further in the morning, and returned to my campsite. I had an idea of what it might be, and lay awake for some time, not being able to fall asleep, so anxious was I for morning to come. Finally sleep did come, and I awoke early with curiosity, excitement, and anticipation.

In the daylight, I studied the single graven line, and sighted down the line in both directions. The left edge of the line pointed toward a nondescript canyon, with no interesting or significant features. To the right however, it was aimed directly to a small flat clearing on the next hill over from where I was standing. Feeling real excitement, I started out for the spot at a trot, anticipating what I might find there.

Exactly in the direction the line on the stone had indicated I found a small clearing at the base of a huge dead and rotting cardon cactus. There was a sunken area, a slight depression in the level of the sandy ground, with a white object projecting up through the surface. I used my hand spade to begin removing the dirt from around what soon proved to be a large animal bone, polished white over the years it had lain there. Working very slowly and carefully, by mid-morning I had succeeded in unearthing the almost intact skeleton of a burro. When the last bones were removed from the pit, I dug down another two feet, but found nothing more.

It was lunch time, so I went back to camp and got a sandwich. I returned to my digging and sat on a rock, eating and thinking. The burro had been buried, obviously, but why? Here in the desert no one normally would have any reason to bury a dead beast like this one. The animals and insects of the desert would have made short work of the carcass. Whoever had taken the time and effort to bury the unfortunate burro must have had a good reason. Could it have been to cover their trail? To avoid drawing attention to the area by attracting swarms of buzzards? Did they perhaps leave something else here too? As I sat, looking around the area, my attention was drawn to another area about 20 feet away from the pit, at the side of a large boulder. It too looked a little sunken, just as the larger one had.

After lunch I turned my attention to this area, and after digging down only a foot or two, struck a plank of rotted ancient wood, which crumbled at my touch. I carefully removed the pieces of wood, and kept digging. I found some rusted and barely recognizable bits of metal, which, after some study I guessed to be the metal fittings of a bridle. There were also bits of rotten leather, and then another layer of the wooden planking, small, as though the remains of a wooden box or crate. I removed what seemed to be the bottom of the box, and decided to keep digging a little further. It is a good thing I did, for only a few inches below the wood my spade hit something hard. I lifted out a blackened oblong metal object, that at first I could not identify. As I removed the dirt and muck, I could see that it was the barrel of a very, very old gun of some kind. Interest piqued, I dug further, and unearthed another metal object. Upon cleaning this one, it became shiny, and I recognized it as being made of silver. When more dirt had been removed, I saw that it was a silver candlestick!

Another three feet of digging yielded no further finds, and as it was getting toward twilight, I returned to camp. After supper, I spent some more time polishing the candlestick to a bright luster. I still have it to this day. It helped me to formulate my theory of the missing treasure of the Jesuits. This was the first tangible evidence I had found, but it fit into place nicely. It helped to validate my ideas, and I vowed to continue the search.

The Missing Jesuit Gold - My Theory

CHAPTER 7

$\mathcal{M}$uch of my time in the Baja, especially in the early days, has been spent around the Mission San Borja. It is a remote spot in the interior of the peninsula, ringed by high mountains. Blessed with a plentiful year-round supply of water from its several springs, it is capable of growing many kinds of crops. It is truly a tranquil and secure place. And, it has gold.

In my opinion, it is not a coincidence that all of the northern mission sites chosen by the Jesuit priests were located in areas rich with gold or silver. Many years ago, when I first came to San Borja, I began to gather as much information as I could about the missions, and used it to help formulate my theory of the "missing" Jesuit gold.

Writings about the Baja for centuries have mentioned the possibility that gold was left behind by the Jesuits when they were expelled in 1767. Historians generally have conceded that the priests undoubtedly had amassed more gold and silver, both in religious icons and bullion, than was found when they departed. I became convinced of this, and formed an idea of what might have happened that I intended to pursue, and hopefully prove true. I will first give you my theory, and then relate some of my own readings and personal experiences that helped me to arrive at these beliefs. This is not meant to be a scholarly rehash of previous writing on the subject. I leave that to others far more adept at research than myself. You will find no footnotes in this book, no lengthy bibliography, no endless citations from other authors. What you will find, are my thoughts, which are based upon research I have carried out for years, and my personal observations in the desert. I have done a lot of reading, a lot of thinking, and a lot of looking around in the hills and valleys where it all took place. It is as much on intuition, careful thought and knowledge of the land that my theory and its supporting evidence rests, as it is on academic research. These are my ideas, and what you read here will be based upon personal experience and secondary sources I have used for background information. I would ask the reader to accept these writings in that light, and on that basis. My theory is as follows:

There actually is a lost treasure left by the departing Jesuit priests. It is NOT in gold or silver bullion, but rather in iconic statuary and holy relics that were sacked from the missions at the time the expulsion took place. These precious objects of gold and silver were spirited away from the missions by ex-soldiers and local mission workers, and hidden in anticipation of being preserved and saved from confiscation. And now, I will tell you what my years of thought and investigation lead me to believe happened and how it all came about.

There still remain in existence many inventories made over the years, of gold and silver objects, most used ceremonially in the missions. Yet these objects were not found when the Jesuits departed the peninsula. I believe there is good reason for their absence. First of all, the Jesuits had a very good surveillance network covering the institutions of Europe, including the crown and the religious orders. Many historians who have written of the period agree that the Jesuits in Baja knew of their impending fate as much as three months before the order was actually given. It then took more time for Galvez and Portola to arrive in the Baja from the mainland, and even more time for them to reach the far-flung missions, of which San Borja was the most northern. By the time the Franciscans got to San Borja de Adac, all they found were stone, clay and wooden replicas of the precious icons mentioned in previous inventories. The real objects were missing. What could have happened to them? It is obvious that the priests could not have taken them. They were closely watched by Portola's soldiers, and there were only sixteen of them expelled. No, for sure this treasure remained somewhere in the vast expanse of the desert. The gold and silver bullion was smuggled out by the industrious Padres during the many years of their dominion over the Indians. The icons remained hidden here in Baja.

It is well known from contemporary accounts that the missions, almost without exception, employed the male Indians under their control in gold mining. In San Borja for instance, hidden mines dating from Jesuit times have been uncovered as far from the mission as Punta Prieta. For decades under the direction of the good Padres, the Indians had worked the mines year-round, not valuing the gold itself, and not being allowed to benefit from finding it. The Indians of Baja did not seek nor use gold as did the Indians of mainland Mexico. Their primary objects of ornamentation came from animals or seashells. Thus they had no reason to hide or withhold any of the gold, and willingly handed it over to the priests.

But what did the priests do with the gold? This is not just a little bit of gold, I believe that the total of that many Indians mining for that long must have been a staggering amount of bullion. I believe that they kept the gold for themselves, and somehow got it transported off the peninsula without the knowledge of the Spanish government.

We do know that the missions themselves, even the most prosperous of them, were not self-supporting. It took a lot of money from other sources to keep them running. The Jesuits were very proficient fund-raisers, and used every avenue of funding available to them. They relied heavily on the Pius Fund, an organized private attempt originated in Spain to provide consistent funding for the missions. They also received individual private gifts and bequests to support their program. Many of these were in the form of religious icons and relics of precious metals for the church altars. After their first few years of existence, the Jesuits reneged on a promise not to require Royal assistance from Spain, and began receiving regular payments from the Crown.

As time went on, more and more of the institutions in Europe began to form suspicions that the Jesuits were not revealing all that was going on in the remote peninsula they inhabited. It was very difficult to check up on them, due both to their remote location, and the fact that they did everything in their power to discourage any type of secular settlement in the Baja. The Jesuits protested loud and long that such secular presence would have a very damaging effect on their work with the natives. They felt non-religious settlers had a very bad influence on their mission Indians. Some in Europe believed them. Others, perhaps less charitable, wondered if perhaps their feelings were based more on a desire not to have all of their activities known.

It was widely suspected for instance, that the missions traded with pirates as well as merchant ships. Given the penchant of the Jesuits for gathering funds from whatever sources they could, this is an understandable suspicion. The majority of the priests were not even Spanish in origin, but came from a number of European countries such as Germany, Italy, and the Netherlands. Their allegiance to the order of Loyola might well have been stronger than their allegiance to the crown, and the gold bullion could easily have been smuggled out to other Jesuit outposts around the world. This was another cause for concern in the Spanish court.

For many years the galleons following the trade route between Mexico and the Philippines needed, and asked for, a port on the west coast of the Baja peninsula. Such a port would afford them safety and refuge from the weather, and especially the English and French pirates that constantly preyed upon them. The Jesuits even received funding for this purpose, but always had one excuse or another why the project could not be undertaken. As the years went by, patience in Madrid grew very thin. With the Russians establishing more and more of a presence in Alta California, Madrid felt the need to push further north to strengthen their claim on the land. The stubborn Jesuits sat in the way of expansion like a cork in a bottle.

At last, the Crown had had enough of the good fathers in Baja, and the order was handed down that they be expelled, and replaced by the Franciscans. It should be noted here that the Jesuit order, founded by the very capable Loyola, was active in much of the known world. There were powerful contingents not only in Europe, but in mainland Mexico and some places in Central and South America as well. They also had many friends in the courts of Europe, especially in Spain. It took more than three months from the time the order was written, until it was carried out. It is very likely that the priests of Baja received word from their European spies in advance of the arrival of Portola's soldiers.

This delay in the carrying out of the expulsion gave the missions time to take some actions before their departure. I believe that among these was the opportunity to seal up and hide all of the active mines the missions had been working. The chief reason for going to all this trouble would be obvious. If such mines were to be discovered, one might be moved to ask the question "So where did all the gold that came from this mine go?" In any event, by the time the order for expulsion reached the missions, the mines had been hidden, and no mention of them was made.

Since going into a hole in the earth and digging out rock all day was not high on the Indians list of fun things to do, it is no wonder they did not mention the mines. As innocent and naïve as they were, they might have reasoned that had they done so, the mines would be reopened, and back to work they would go. A good number of these previously worked mines have been found. Of these, some produced good amounts of gold and silver a hundred years later. The vast majority have remained unfound to this day. This is yet another reason to carefully explore the desert of central Baja.

So where did the gold and silver that these mines produced go? I believe that some of it was used by the Padres in barter for needed supplies. In my opinion, the vast majority of it was shipped in ingot form to other Jesuit missions in Europe and South America. There has been speculation with some corroborating evidence in recently discovered secret communications of that period that the Jesuits at least briefly considered setting up an empire in Paraguay. Some of the bullion could have been directed there, Spain being none the wiser.

One very strong piece of evidence for this theory is the fact that after the expulsion of the Jesuits, Franciscan missionaries discovered a gold ingot buried in the sand on the beaches of Bahia de los Angeles. The Franciscans, perhaps to show their honesty to the Crown, and draw a distinction between their loyalty and that of the departed Jesuits, immediately reported the find to Spain. It seems to me the logical question to be asked is: "Where did that come from?" It did not carry any stamp identifying it as property of the Crown, as all legitimate ingots did in that period. Pirates did not normally make it up the gulf that far north. Even if they had, their gold was all stolen, and would have had the official stamps. No, the only feasible explanation was, and still is, that this gold was lost by the Jesuits during transport to other venues. And thus I arrive at a very important part of my theory of the lost treasure of the Jesuits. There is no treasure to be found in gold or silver bullion. It did indeed exist, but was all successfully spirited away by the very efficient and skilled Jesuit fathers.

But does this mean there is no treasure left by the Jesuits? Not at all. They had not the time, means, or inclination to desecrate their beloved churches by sacking the ceremonial relics of gold and silver that had been largely donated by patrons in Europe. I believe, and have ample personal evidence to bolster that belief, that these works of art were stolen by locals, largely soldiers and secular settlers. I further believe that this theft took place between the time that the Jesuits left, and possession of the missions was completed by the soldiers of Portola and Galvez, long before the arrival of the Franciscans. This is the final, and most important aspect of my theory.

Such objects, once stolen, would be immediately recognized locally, so had no value in Baja other than to be melted down into ingots. This would have been easy to do, but I do not think that is what happened, for the following reasons. Even if the objects had been reduced to ingots, some explanation would be required locally as to where they originated. Not having a believable answer could easily lead to confiscation of the gold, and perhaps incarceration of the person that had it. No, even in ingot form, it would have had to be taken to some distant place to be redeemed.

The altar statuary was another matter completely. The Jesuits had convinced their followers that these objects were sacred, and to be revered as having holy status, befitting of the highest reverence. With the Order of Loyola leaving, what would become of these objects? Would they be taken away? Would the altars be desecrated by some new order that might occupy the church, with differing ideas of the sacred? In this, it would seem that such fears had valid basis, as it was made abundantly clear to the incoming order of Franciscans that complete cooperation with the crown was expected, and would be enforced. I believe that these objects were taken from the mission at San Borja by the faithful among them, to be preserved and kept from seizure. Who else would have taken the time to replace almost all the missing objects with similar ones made of stone, wood, or clay?

Any book on the history of Baja one picks up takes great pains to paint as naive the idea of hidden treasure from the Jesuits. They deride the concept as wishful thinking and idle conjecture with no basis in fact. They despair at the damage done to old mission walls by those treasure seekers who have torn them apart looking for gold bars. In this aspect, I agree with them. There is no buried wealth in the form of bullion. The treasure consists of relics taken from the church altars not for profit, but for preservation, by well-meaning and pious people. This is especially likely in the more remote northern missions such as San Borja

This then, is my theory of the missing gold of the Jesuits. In the chapters that follow, I will talk of my life in Baja California, my decades of prospecting, and stories of Bahia de Los Angeles. I will also attempt to expand on my ideas of what happened to the holy relics that came up missing. The final decision as to the accuracy of my theory I will leave up to the reader.

The "Shining Dawn"

CHAPTER 8

$\mathcal{G}$old. It is truly amazing stuff. It came into my life early, grabbed me hard, and has held me tight all my days since. From that first trip into the Nevada goldfields with my Uncle when I was just a little boy, it has been my obsession, my passion, my profession, and my mistress. And I am not unique in this regard. Throughout history, mankind has been seeking and honoring gold, valuing it beyond all other metals, and even raising it to the status of an object of religious worship. I felt from an early age that if I was to spend my life in quest of this precious substance, I had better learn something about it.

I found that gold is what is called a "Noble" metal. That means it often occurs in nature in its pure state and is very resistant to corrosion or oxidation. It is without doubt the first metal ever to be used by man, and such use is lost in antiquity. According to scholars, long before man used iron or copper, while natural rock was the only common tool, he sought, used, and revered gold. I can certainly understand that, because there are several reasons why it, above all metals, would be selected for use by man.

Firstly, as anyone who has ever unearthed a nugget will attest, it has natural beauty! After millions of years in the ground, it emerges shiny and glistening, and usually the beautiful color of the sun. Even among primitive men, there was a natural proclivity to see beauty in nature. Such beautiful things as shells, feathers, butterfly wings – and gold, were valued by our ancient progenitors, and often used as decoration, adornment or symbols of status, authority, or nobility.

Secondly, gold is relatively soft, malleable, and easy to make into different shapes. It could easily be made into necklaces, ear or nose rings, or later into objects of worship. From these humble beginnings come both the gilded bust of Nephertiti, and the dome of the Basilica of St. Johns, and thousands of man's most noble and esteemed artistic efforts that we see around us today.

Finally, it is rare. Mankind has a natural tendency to value that which is hard to attain. I don't think I have ever met a woman who hadn't at some point in her life learned this lesson! As I said, gold is my mistress, and in her own way she teases me and makes me want her as much as any woman ever has. I would imagine that if the first primitive man had worn a gold necklace, and it had been admired, it would have lost a lot of its value if the next day all of his caveman neighbors had appeared wearing a similar one!

Suffice it to say that no one knows, or ever will know, when gold was first used by primitive peoples. It happened too long ago, and before any semblance of history had been recorded in even its most rudimentary sense. What IS certain is that it has been used ever since in an increasing variety of ways, and is as important and as valued today as it ever was.

The first recorded records of human history that do exist mention prominently the use and veneration of gold. It is observed in all ancient cultures that have left a record of their beginnings. As man rose inexorably through the Paleolithic, Mesolithic and Neolithic eras and learned to plant seeds and raise animals for food, gold and its uses emerged and proliferated with him. The earliest recorded societies such as the Sumerian or Egyptian are replete with references to gold, and the high esteem in which it was held. The beautiful yellow metal was worshipped as an earthly representative of the sun. The Egyptian culture saw it as the embodiment of purity and virtue. It was along the Nile that the custom of the gold wedding ring was born, as well as the custom of wearing it on the third finger of the left hand. The Egyptians thought that there was a vein that led from this finger directly to the heart. I'll bet you didn't realize how romantic those ancient Egyptians could be!

It would be impossible to recount here all the uses of, and reverence for gold among the Greeks and Romans. The symbol for gold in chemistry is "AU". This is derived from the Latin word "Aurum", which translates to "shining dawn", and gave rise to their creation of the beautiful Aurora, Roman goddess of the dawn. The Romans tied gold to their very concept of the future.

The Greek story of Jason and the Golden Fleece is actually an allegory, and is, in fact, a reference to gold mining. By the time of the Greeks, men had been struggling for thousands of years to improve their methods of finding gold. At first, of course, it was found by merely seeing a beautiful flash of yellow in a stream, or an outcropping of rock. Then, as its worth became greater, all that was easily found had been taken. It was necessary to begin searching for it beneath the surface of the earth, and panning and mining had its beginnings. By the time of the Greeks, the state of the art in gold collection had risen to the point that animal hides were often used to strain the last few tiny grains of gold from the black sands in which it is often found. Hides, usually goats or sheep (a fleece) were used to strain the sands. The water bearing the grains of gold was poured carefully through the fleece, which was then put in the sun to dry. When dried, it was shaken, and the tiniest specks of gold could be collected on a polished surface. The search for the Golden Fleece was really the search for these skins, which indicated a rich gold strike!

After the fall of Rome, gold collection continued to be practiced and improved upon in virtually every civilized country in which gold is found in appreciable quantities. Every country in Europe had its miners, and as the gold that was easiest to collect disappeared, newer and more effective methods were found to perpetuate the supply. In England, the name "gold" was derived from the Saxon "gelo", meaning yellow. During the dark ages the progress in improved methods was slow, but steady. With the coming of the Renaissance however, it took a great leap forward, propelled by all the coincidental discoveries in the science and technology of the time.

Probably the best miners of them all were the Spanish. They had developed advanced techniques for the time in their quest for precious gemstones, with which their country had been generously endowed by nature. This would stand them in good stead indeed when they made their attempt to unlock the riches of the new world. Some of the best mining practices of Europe came to the Baja with the Jesuit occupation.

Today, the value of gold has continued to increase. More ways are found to use it. There may be some in your teeth – there is in mine. Its unique properties have seen it become a mainstay in space travel. Above your head right now, there are tons of gold circling the earth night and day. There is gold on the moon, put there by man. There may be gold in your car, your appliances, or your electronic equipment. Gold is so versatile that it can be squeezed into layers so thin they are only a few molecules thick.

It is estimated that all the gold that has been found by man since the dawn of history could be contained in a 50 foot square cube! And, gold is seldom wasted or lost. Of all the metals known to man, there is a higher percentage of gold remaining in use from the total amount that has been found.

I am not alone in my obsession and love for gold. This wonderful metal has had me in its spell all my life. It has been good to me.

Jesuit Gold -
My Search Begins

*D*uring all of my years in the central Baja desert, when I am in the mountains I am actually looking for two things. First, I am looking for gold. I am good enough at finding it, having been at it for such a long time that I am usually successful in this endeavor. My second purpose is to find clues to the hiding places of the icons that disappeared from the San Borja mission at the time of the Jesuit expulsion. For many years I was not successful in this quest, but I never gave up hope, or trying, and continued to believe in my theory as to the fate of these relics.

At my home in Bahia de los Angeles, I would pore over topographical maps of the desert and mountains north of San Borja. Which path would the people taking out the treasure likely have chosen?   Would they have taken the well traveled roads through Green Valley? Probably not. They would not have wanted to risk detection, and most likely would have used the harder, but less frequented rough trails through the mountains. When planning my next prospecting trip, I always took this search into consideration.

I felt that the cache taken from the churches, if it existed at all, would be somewhere to the north of San Borja, the northernmost of the Jesuit missions. This area was also the part of the Baja mountains that were richest in gold, so it was convenient to kill two birds with one stone. While I was looking for the telltale signs of gold deposits, I was also on the lookout for any signs of Jesuit presence, such as wagon wheel ruts, or objects which they may have abandoned on their journey. It was primarily for this reason, but for finding gold as well, that in later years I always carried my metal detector with me when I went into the mountains.

When I prepared for a prospecting trip, I developed a set routine. I would first look over my maps and decide which general area I wished to search. Then I would begin to gather the tools, supplies and materials I would need, and load them into my pickup truck. I took food and water, a tarp for shade, a chair, pots and pans for cooking, and all of the equipment I would use for my prospecting.

If I was going to look for placer gold, as well as hardrock nuggets, I would take my drywasher. The Mexicans called this device a "Pom – Pom", because of the sound it made when being operated. This device is the principal tool for separating gold grains from the desert sand. In the Baja, miners do not have the luxury of abundant water as did the 49'ers in California. If water is available, as it was in Sacramento, it can be used with high pressure hoses to dig away the dirt and mud to get at the gold. It can also be used to build sluice boxes, or to "Pan" the gold, a process using the well known gold pan and water to separate the heavy gold from the lighter worthless rock and sand. But in the Baja, there was almost never enough water around for these techniques. We had to use what is called "Dry panning", or separating the gold using methods other than water.

The drywasher, or Pom-Pom was our most essential tool for placer mining. Essentially, this is a very dependable device which uses air, rather than water, to separate the gold from the sand in which it is found. It does this extremely well. In the hands of an experienced operator, it can separate sand particles so small they are barely visible to the human eye. These specks are very light individually, but there are many more of them than the larger pieces, and they must be removed in order to separate the gold. The tiny specs of gold thus sorted make the bulk of gold the average placer miner finds. There is no quantity of gold too insignificant to be bothered with. Placer mining is a process of slow but steady accrual, and attention to detail is essential. The drywasher is the heart of this process.

This remarkable machine at about 25 pounds is light enough to be carried almost anywhere a man can walk in the desert or mountains. It uses air pressure rather than water to do its work. The basic machine has a wooden frame with legs that allow it to be put on the ground and operated at waist level from a standing position. Under the frame is a central bellows, with a crankshaft and a crank. The riffle board a flat, slanted plank with ridges like a washboard, is placed on top of the bellows. Clamps on each side of the riffle board hold it tightly onto a rubber gasket which makes the bellows air tight. The bellows itself is designed so that when it is cranked down, a valve opens allowing air to enter on this initial down stroke. Continuing the cranking motion brings the bellow back upward, closing the valve. The air is compressed and blown upward from underneath the raw ore, through a cloth layer, usually made of unbleached muslin. The airflow is regulated so that the lighter particles of sand are blown clear, leaving only the heaviest materials to be further separated.

There is a hopper at the top of the dry washer that will hold about two and a half cubic feet of ore. Above this is a screen tilted down at one edge. This screen filters out the larger rocks as you fill the hopper. They fall to the ground and do not enter the hopper bag. The bottom of the bag has a small feed tube that can be opened or closed to control the flow of material into the riffle board. The ore is blown from below and the lighter material is carried down the tilted riffle board by gravity, filling each riffle as it goes. When it gets to the bottom riffle, it is then lost over the side and down onto the ground. The heavier material, which contains the gold, also moves down the riffle board, but at a slower pace. When it gets to the bottom riffle, no more material is allowed to enter, and the blowing stops while the black sand and gold is scooped out for further culling. I usually collected this high grade "black sand" in containers, and took it back to my home in Bahia to undergo final processing into pure gold.

If I wanted only to do a sample of the black sand, to test the quality of my find, I would use a little bit of water in my horn to further process the ore. The horn was from a cow, and had been carved into a scoop-like tool. I could use small amounts of water, a sort of mini-wet panning, just to test the worth of the sample. If I saw significant color, it would be worth further processing.

The final processing of this placer gold was accomplished in the old days by using that wonderful element mercury. This fascinating metal is liquid at room temperatures, and is the gold miner's best friend. It has an affinity for gold, and the remarkable ability to absorb it. The gold goes into the mercury and is trapped there until heated. Because of this, all successful miners of the time used the mercury process for purifying their ore.

This is the way the process worked. I would use some porous vegetable, usually a potato as they were readily available, cheap, and worked well. After using the mercury to absorb as much gold as it could from any given sample, I would hollow out the potato, and pour in the mercury. Then I would put the potato in a pan of water over a fire. Since mercury is a highly volatile metal, it would evaporate very quickly, and be taken up by the potato. The gold, requiring a far higher temperature to evaporate, would be left behind. When the potato was taken off of the fire, a little shining pellet of gold would remain. That was the miner's reward for going through the whole process. Gold obtained by this method constituted the bulk of my income, far more than the nuggets I found. When the potato and water mixture cooled, the mercury fell to the bottom in drops. It could then be reclaimed for further use.

My days in the desert settled into a predictable routine. Rising early, usually before the sun had appeared, my first task was to make hot coffee and fix a breakfast. Then I would either begin my work at once, or pack up everything needed and strike off in the desert to find a likely spot to begin the refining process. I would then do any digging I needed to do, and fill up the hopper on the drywasher and go to work. Around noon I would usually eat a lunch, something that didn't need to be cooked. If I felt like it, as I often did, I would take a short siesta in the shade. Then I would work until near dark, return to my camp, and make supper. This was always the most elaborate meal of the day, and I was usually very hungry after long hours of work. After a large and filling supper, it was time to clean any pots and dishes or silverware I had used. As water was very hard to come by, I usually did the washing with dry sand. It works well.

Then came a time of the day that I loved, - the evening. I would build a fire, let it burn down, and just sit and stare into the coals, thinking. I always carried a bottle of tequila with me, (and kept a stash in my truck as well) for medical use in case of snakebites. If there had been no snake bites that day, I always figured that the tequila was, at that point extra, and I had better get rid of it so I would have less to carry around. I would mix it with some fruit juice and drink it while sitting at the fire. I always carried a canvas chair with arms in my truck for my evening sessions by these cheerful fires. All my life I have been a firm believer that chairs with arms are much better to relax in than chairs without arms. This is especially true after a hard day of using the drywasher.

As I would sit and stare at the flames, and sip my tequila, I would think of how many before me had done the same things on this lonely stretch of desert. My mind would often wander back to the time of the Indians or the first explorers who sat under the same stars watching their own fires so many years ago. We would share the loneliness, the solitude, and the quiet beauty of the desert together, across the many years, and even centuries, between us. I have never been uncomfortable or afraid of being alone, and I enjoyed the extreme privacy of a solitary existence on the desert. I had lots of friends and acquaintances back in Bahia de los Angeles, and I enjoyed being with them, and in what measures of civilization the little town could afford. But I loved my time alone in the desert too, and enjoyed every day of it.

I also loved the daily solving of the puzzle. Where has the desert hidden its gold? Can I find enough clues to lead me to it? Tomorrow I might work all day and have little or nothing to show for it. Or, if I was skillful enough to solve the puzzle, I might find sufficient gold in one day to finance a trip to Las Vegas, and enjoy a week at the gambling tables in those crystal chandeliered palaces that I love so much. Besides the Baja, the place that I love the most in this world is, ironically, in the middle of another desert. I have so many wonderful memories of my childhood in Las Vegas, and have spent a lifetime generating other wonderful memories of a more adult nature there.

Most of the money I have made from the gold I found over the years has gone to family and friends. I have kept very little for myself, because I prefer to live a simple lifestyle, and possessions have not meant a lot to me. The life I like to live does not require a lot of money. I live on the beach in a beautiful place, yet pay little rent. I have a pickup truck which I have replaced every few years, and is the most expensive thing I own. I have no telephone, belong to no country clubs, don't play golf, go to the theatre, or feel the need to impress anyone with my financial net worth. I have given much money over my life to people that needed it, with no expectation of getting it back. Any excess funds I might have had from particularly lucky finds I have made over the years have gone to my favorite vice – gambling in Las Vegas. A kilo of gold taken from an ancient riverbed in the Baja means a week on Fremont street for me. If I should happen to get lucky there, as has happened, the week might turn into a month, spent with temporary friends more than happy to help me spend my money.

I realize that this would not be a lifestyle approved by many of the more traditional souls that might be reading these words, but it was one that suited me well. I have no boss, punch no clocks, work where and when I please, and only IF I please. My lifestyle has been one of freedom, enjoyment of the many things of true value life has to offer, and above all, I have lived close to nature. Although I like being in a soft bed with pillows and sheets, always warm and dry at home, I could not live my life that way all the time. I would miss the desert skies at night so beautifully full of stars, or the sweetness of a Spring morning, hiking through a meadow bright with desert flowers. I love living as one with the creatures and plants of the desert, in complete freedom of movement, and of thought, and of life. I feel no need for approval then, nor do I now.

All of this is impossible to relate to the many who conclude that since I do not drive an expensive car, live in a multi-million dollar house, or belong to an exclusive country club, that I must not have found much gold. That is the life they would choose to lead, and one that I would find as shallow and fatuous as I do these individuals themselves. Trying to explain my values to them would be useless. It would be like trying to teach a pig to sing – it would waste my time, and annoy the pig. So, I let them think what they will, as I have found it a meaningless enterprise to try to convince them of anything. In this book, however, I am laying my soul bare for all to see. I am telling you about my life, and how I have lived it. Take from these chapters what you will dear reader, and leave the rest behind.

The Curious Case of the Missing Cocaine

CHAPTER 10

$\mathcal{T}$ he morning was beautiful, as mornings usually are in Bahia de los Angeles. I was sitting at the table on the patio in front of my beachfront casita, watching as the sun rose higher above the bay islands into the clear blue sky. I looked forward to another lazy, comfortable day, relaxing and enjoying the springtime weather. Little did I know that this was not to be. The coffee tasted very good, as Mexican coffee does, and I was just about ready for my second cup when the town Delegado, Jose-Luis walked down the dirt driveway from Guillermo's restaurant and onto my patio.

"Muy Buenos Dias Senor Heel!"

"¿Buenos Jose-Luis, que paso?"

The Delegado seemed a little excited for such a laid back morning, and I realized why as he began to explain things to me. It seemed that someone coming in to town from Punta Prieta that morning had reported that a rather large, twin engine cargo airplane had been landed on the Agua Amargua dry lakebed about 12 miles northwest of town. No one had been seen around the plane, but the Delegado was concerned that there might be injured passengers, or some one needing assistance. He asked me to accompany him to the site, to assist with administering whatever help might be needed. I agreed to go, and soon we were on the road in the Delgado's ancient pickup truck, heading toward Amargua.

Sure enough, the plane was there, easy to see from the road. It looked in pretty good shape, and obviously had been landed under control. I recognized it as a vintage Convair 440, a sturdy and reliable cargo carrier from the 1940's. Many of these planes were still in use, and had proven themselves to be real workhorses, capable of hauling very heavy loads. The landing gear were all intact, save for one blown tire. We pulled up next to the airplane and got out. We called out with no answer. There were three sets of footprints clearly visible in the sand, heading toward the main road.

The Delegado climbed inside the plane, and confirmed that it had indeed been abandoned. I noticed that the right engine was covered with oil. I moved the pickup truck under the nose of the plane, and removed the oil soaked cowling from the engine. The whole bottom of the engine block had broken out, and it was obvious that the engine had blown a piston and seized up tight. Whoever had been flying that plane must have been one hell of a pilot to land it safely with one engine, at night, on a lakebed with no lights, and quite possibly a very stiff cross wind as well.

I heard Jose-Luis call me from within the plane, so I climbed inside to see what he had found. He was standing in the cargo bay, holding a plastic wrapped bag of white powder about the size of a small loaf of bread. Behind him were several bales of such bags, many hundreds of them. Cocaine! Suddenly everything became clear - what the plane was doing there, and the rapid disappearance of the crew. Jose-Luis and I talked over how to handle this situation. We decided that he would return to town and call the State and Federal authorities in Guerrero Negro. It was the closest town with any Federal offices. In the meantime, I would stay at the landing site, and watch over the precious cargo. He jumped into the pickup, and sped off toward the road, sending a giant cloud of dust behind him, marking his rapid progress across the lakebed.

As I stood there in the plane on the silent lakebed, the seriousness of my situation began to dawn on me. I was alone, unarmed, and standing between whoever might arrive on the scene and a fortune in drugs.

"Herman," I thought, "this is not one of the smartest things you have ever done in your life!"

What if the drug dealers return with a truck to haul out their powdery cargo? This, in my mind, was a distinct possibility, given its remoteness and the fact that the crew had had many hours in which to enlist the aid of their henchmen whom might be nearby. They certainly would not want to leave any witnesses behind, and I was as good as dead if they did arrive on the scene. The vast expanse of dry lakebed lay absolutely flat in all directions around the plane. There was almost no plant life due to the high salt content of the sand. There was no place to run and hide, and even if I left now, my footprints would be easy to follow. No, I decided, my only chance was to stay with the plane, and hope whoever arrived first was friend rather than foe. I really would have preferred to be seated back at my house, on my third cup of coffee!

After a long and anxious wait, I was relieved to see the Delgado's truck approaching, followed by two other pickups full of local townspeople he had recruited for guard duty. They were all armed, with an odd assortment of rifles, shotguns, pistols, and supported by an array of machetes, knives and clubs. A ragtag group to be sure, but one I was confident could, by its size alone, deter any rescue attempt the drug dealers might have in mind for their lost cargo. Jose-Luis informed me that he had contacted the authorities as planned, and they had told him to guard the site well, and wait for their arrival. Jose-Luis had decided it would be best to inventory the cargo of drugs, and had enlisted the aid of Vascillio who ran the grocery store in town. Vascillio had brought his grocery scale for this purpose, and immediately began weighing each bag of cocaine, with the local school teacher dutifully recording its weight.

The task of weighing each of the several hundred packages took considerable time. When it was completed, Lalo Perez, the school teacher carefully totaled up the weight for each package. An anxious group of volunteer guards crowded into the cargo hold, curious to know how much cocaine there was. Lalo felt the gravity of the moment, and the rapt attention he commanded. He began, very officially, and in a loud and authoritative voice. "Amigos, the grand total of the weight of the cocaine is..........." The anticipation was palpable in the crowded cargo hold.

"Exactly........." Everyone leaned forward to hear.

"............. 1080 Kilos!"

The assembled men reacted excitedly to the dramatic announcement. There were whistles, and shouts of "¡Hijole!," " ¡Madre mia!," and

"¡Caramba!" This was indeed stunning news, as the value of this amount of cocaine was greater than the total value of the entire pueblo, and the lifetime earnings of all of its inhabitants combined.

To a man, the brave little group in the plane realized the importance of their duty to guard such a treasure. Their shared a determination to defend the fortune by force if necessary. Some checked their guns; others tested the blades of their machetes for sharpness. They all settled in to wait for assistance from the Estado or Federales, or to repel any return of the *drogeros*. I felt certain at that point that any attempt by the drug runners to reclaim their lost possessions would be met with a vigorous defense.

By late afternoon, the first official vehicles arrived from Guerrero Negro. There were both State and Federal officers, followed very shortly by a contingent of trucks bearing Mexican Army troops. All of us who had preserved the plane felt very proud. We had played a very crucial role in something of great importance. The head *honcho* of both the Federal and State police, as well as the ranking officer from the Army, thanked us for our vigilance. They also made it very clear that not only were they now in charge, but our continued presence at the scene was no longer needed, and indeed would not be allowed, now, or in the future. This was a crime scene, and local people would no longer be permitted near it. Vascillio showed the newly arrived junta his tally sheet showing the phenomenal amount of cocaine that had been inventoried. The papers with his figures were confiscated on the spot.

"We will need this for the investigation", we were told, "and any other information you may have recorded as well."

They asked us if any photographs of the cocaine had been taken, but none of us had brought a camera. Once again we were thanked, and told that we now could, and should, leave and go back to town.

For the next several days, the plane and its cargo were the primary, and almost the sole topic of conversation in the town. Some of the citizens of Bahia wondered aloud if we would be given some sort of a reward, or be accorded some honor. Others predicted a letter of appreciation from the *Presidente* himself. None of this was forthcoming however. One day Pancho Galvez arrived back from Guerrero Negro with a newspaper in his hands. Pancho was a hard-working rancher who had never been to school, and could not read well enough to understand the news he was bringing. He did recognize the name of Bahia de los Angeles in the large title of the story on the front page. He sent several people out to look for the Delegado to read the article aloud. News of the paper's arrival spread fast, and soon a crowd of townspeople had gathered around Pancho's car. The Delegado arrived, along with almost everyone living within a two mile radius, and began to read the article aloud. The crowd stood around him in excited anticipation. Would they indeed be given a reward for finding such a valuable thing? Would their heroic role in the preservation of the plane and it's cargo be acknowledged?

The Delegado began reading the story in a very loud voice so all could hear.

"The headline says 'Police Seize Cocaine near Bahia de los Angeles.'"

There was a murmur of approval from the crowd. At least their village had been mentioned in a headline, for the first time any of them could remember. Jose-Luis continued:

"Federal Police today announced that after a long investigation and much effort, they had managed to intercept an airplane loaded with cocaine near the town of Bahia de los Angeles." The assemblage was confused at this.

Reuben Carasco called out "Hey, THEY didn't find the stuff, WE did!" The entire group voiced agreement with this assessment.

"Ok, listen!" the Delegado continued. "Government officials say the 280 Kilos of cocaine found on the plane was the largest single seizure of drugs ever recorded in Baja California."

At this point the crowd disintegrated into pandemonium.

Vascillio shouted "It was not a mere 280 kilos, it was 1080 kilos. I weighed it with my own scale!" Some of the villagers had long suspected the accuracy of his scale, but not to this extent.

"I added up all the bags!" said Lalo, "They are lying!"

"Does it say anything about a reward for us?" Carmela Murillo screamed at the Delegado.

Jose-Luis could only shake his head, "No, no reward."

Prieto Garza yelled above the crowd "Did the Presidente say anything about us guarding the plane?"

Jose-Luis again shook his head in the negative. At this point the people of Bahia de los Angeles had heard enough, and were no longer interested in the rest of the story. They were angry, and left, mumbling and muttering, many making silent vows to abandon the PRI and vote PAN in the next election.

In the days following the newspaper article, there was much speculation about the whereabouts of the missing 800 kilos of cocaine. Some blamed the Federales, others the State police, and a smaller group suspected the military. Some thought that all three might have been temporary partners in the situation. But, no investigation was ever launched, as all the original reports listed the lower number of kilos. The only thing that everyone agreed upon was that it was they, not the government who had found the plane. If anyone deserved to profit from the affair, it was them. They had guarded the plane at the risk of their lives, and had not removed even one bag. Not only did they get no recompense, the village was never accorded a good word of thanks for their good deeds from anyone, much less a letter from El Presidente. Jose Luis shook his head, and muttered, "It is true what they say. In Mexico the law is like a spider's web. It catches the little flies, like us amigos, but the big birds, they fly right through it."

Except for the one engine, the plane was in pretty good shape. Several weeks later, a team of mechanics from the Mexican army, assisted by technicians from the Aero Mexico Airlines, managed to replace the engine and blown tire. With a professional airline pilot at the controls, the plane successfully took off from the lakebed, circled above the town to gain altitude, and disappeared to the north. For years the abandoned parts of the engine and the blown tire lay on the lakebed marking the spot where it all happened. I think they are probably still there. Where the missing cocaine went is anybody's guess.

Here I am, full of hope and dreams in 1940. This is my Seaman's certification.

The first glimpse of Bahia de los Angeles is a thrilling sight.

I rarely did any hard rock mining. This picture shows my partner and I as we follow a pretty good vein into the mountain.

Antero Diaz was a friendly man by nature, but a man of much strength and determination, worthy of respect. He was not a man to cross.

I asked this guy where the gold was buried, but he wasn't talking!

Mission San Javier, in a beautiful palm oasis with a fresh water river.

When metal detectors came along, they were a big help. Here I am doing my favorite thing – starting out on a trip through my beloved central Baja desert.

Antero Diaz and his wife Cruz with big yellowtails and a grouper.

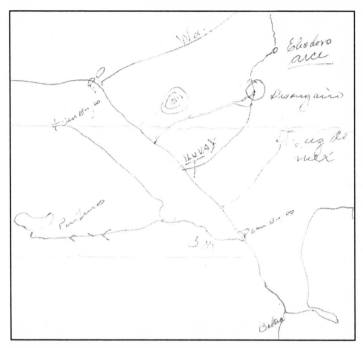

This is a map Antero Diaz drew for me. It shows some of the mines near Bahia de los Angeles.

I am about to lead a group of some local men on a trek into the desert to count game animals.

Mining - Art Versus Science

I have had a lifetime to reflect on the state of the art of mining, or is it perhaps more accurately said the state of the science?   I think like so many things in life, it encompasses elements of both. Each individual who is involved in it, or studies it, decides for him or her self how much of each is involved. Sometimes they overlap. At other times they become indistinguishable from one another.

I like to think of the analogy of the two ship captains, both of whom are able to accurately predict a storm. The ship captain that uses science will use everything at his command to maximize the accuracy of his prediction. He will read charts, take temperature and pressure readings, analyze the flow and direction of the wind, and in these days, even consult a computer based weather station relayed by satellite to his ship. He tends to be the younger of the two, more dependent on science and tools, and more educated in a formal sense. He compiles and analyzes all of the relevant data he can find, and based upon this, he predicts a storm is likely. He only knows what his instruments tell him.

The second captain uses the art of seamanship. He comes up on deck, looks around, feels the air, breathes it in, studies the sea, the clouds, the horizon, and concludes that there will be a storm. He is in agreement with his colleague who used scientific methodology, but for completely different reasons. He usually has more experience on the water than his counterpart, has less formal learning but more ability to apply practically the intuitive information he can gather. He may not even be aware, for instance, that he has noted the birds flying in a certain direction, or the ever so slightly different sound of the lapping of the waves on the hull of the ship, but knows instinctively from past voyages that what he sees, hears, smells, and feels often foretells a storm. He could not tell you precisely why he knows, but he does know that there will be a storm.

It is the same with mining. I would be very foolish if I didn't use all the tools available to me to find the greatest amount of gold possible. There are many things I can borrow from science to make my job easier and more productive. For instance, since their availability, I almost always take a metal detector with me when I am prospecting. This certainly is one of the gifts of science. And there is mercury, and Geographic Positioning Systems (GPS). I would be remiss not to take advantage of these new devices. But I will also put to use all of the experience I have accumulated over the years, and apply the "art" of mining that my years in the desert have afforded me. I would be counterproductive to do otherwise.

When I enter a new part of the desert, for instance, subconsciously I can relate it to countless others I have seen over the years. I know which places are likely to be a waste of effort, and which have a better chance of paying off. I know this because of the countless times I have either failed to find gold, or have been fortunate enough to find a good placer or hard rock source. Like the old sea captain, I might not be able to tell you exactly why I would choose one place over another, but I know I would be right as often as my counterpart who uses satellite photos, magnetic anomaly detection, seismology, and a host of recent scientific methods beyond the ability of a lone prospector. Both are useful, both have their advantages, and neither one is dominant at this point over the other.

Another decision I made early on in my lifetime of mining is to work alone. At times, I have prospected with a partner, but never have I worked as part of a large mining operation. History is replete with examples of men being forced to labor in mines, doing backbreaking work in the most dangerous of situations. In the early days, the work was almost always been done by forced labor, slaves or convicted criminals condemned to risk their lives so that others might profit. That was almost always the case in Spain, and when the Spaniards came to the new world, they brought the evil habit with them. The English came wanting land, and moved the Indians off it. The French came wanting to trade, and worked with the Indians rather than subjugating them. The Spanish wanted the gold and silver, and used the Indians to get it. Many an Indian suffered greatly in the mines at the hands of the Spanish, on both secular and religious projects. As we shall see, the Jesuit priests were not above forcing the Indian men to toil in the mines, only to hand over what they produced.

No, being a cog in a giant wheel that turns day after day, year after year to produce gold and winding up with only a salary as a reward for my effort was not for me. I preferred to work alone, and all the gold I found, I kept for myself. Using all the benefits of science that are available to the present day prospector, as well as the wealth of experience I have built up over the years, has allowed me to find more than my share of Baja gold. And I did it while roaming free, with the desert as my home, and the desert animals as my companions. I had no boss, no prescribed work week, took vacations when I damned well pleased, and have I mentioned it? I found gold. By now you know better than to ask me how much. Let's just say that I have always had the money to pay for what I wanted, and many a visit to the casinos in Las Vegas to boot. It has been a good life, a long life, a life of my own choice, and one lived for the most part free and in a beautiful place, the central Baja desert.

My Fall at Yubay

$\mathcal{T}$ he vast majority of the time I have spent in the desert, I have been alone. I much prefer to be by myself, and have always felt there were many advantages in not being part of a group, or even in the company of one other person. For one thing, it allows me to make, and carry out, all my own decisions. I do not need to consult with or come to agreement with any other person. I can set my own limits, and find my own preferred position on the scale between safety and achievement. I and I alone decide the proper mixture of risk and reward on every plan I make. I like it that way.

Secondly, I like the special bond between the desert and me when I am alone. I am free without distraction to try my best to become one with my surroundings, to assimilate myself into the realm of nature as an equal partner. I love to concentrate on noting even the smallest details, and to learn from them all I can about the wonderful places I am constantly exploring. I find that maintaining this level of concentration is much easier if I am by myself. And the scale of things to observe in the Baja desert is immense. The mountains, the seas around them, and the sky above all seem massive and inscrutable, defying complete understanding, aloof and unobtainable. But with an increased familiarity with all of these things, they become accessible if they are studied closely. The giant mountains are all made up of a kaleidoscope of bits of stone and earth and sand, each of which can be investigated and noted. Enough of these instances of examination of the minutia can lead to a global understanding of the entire mountain, and how it exists and is constantly changing. The same is true of the sea, and the sky. It is vigorous and consistent study of detail that leads to the basic knowledge of all the things that make up the world in which we live, and as we know it. I have always thought it was a shame that most people on earth never get the chance to delve into these secrets to the extent that my life in the desert has allowed me to do. I am determined to continue to learn more deeply about these things until the day I die.

Lastly, and most importantly, when I am alone in the desert, any gold I might find and take out with me, is mine and mine alone. The location of any gold I discover but cannot take out with me is known to me and only me. I can come back for it when I am able, with the reasonable expectation that it will still be there upon my return. As the number of miners having such knowledge increases, the likelihood of maintaining secrecy diminishes, usually to near zero. As mentioned elsewhere in this book, there are valid reasons why a prospector must keep some information to himself. Any miner who does not do this, soon learns his lesson the hard way. That is why I have met few desert rats such as myself that do not know and honor the law of not asking nor answering certain types of questions. As you read this book, and certain things are not discussed in complete detail, you will understand why. Ok? Remember that 'miners' law'!

In spite of these very powerful incentives for going it alone in the desert, doing so sends the needle on the risk-reward gauge skewed to the risk side. One could contemplate a thousand things that might constitute an emergency on any prospecting trip, and a thousand more that are beyond contemplation. There are plants and animals aplenty that can injure or poison one in the desert. There is the relentless sun, and the constant threat of thirst and dehydration if anything happens to your water supply. There are cliffs to fall from, potential cave-ins when digging to bedrock, spines that can puncture shoes or even tires. And finally, and with perhaps as much lethal potential as any of these, there is your fellow man.

Meeting anyone when you are alone in the desert entails an element of danger. You might meet a miner such as yourself, or a harmless hiker on vacation from the United States or even Europe. It could just as easily be some one who is interested in the gold you have found, or a drug runner you have stumbled upon by accident. They know full well that if they kill you, and hide your body, it might be years, if ever, before you are found. The risk is very small to them, and the upside can be considerable. To help shift the odds a little more in my favor, I made it a habit from my earliest days in the Baja to carry a handgun with me at all times. It did not guarantee my survival, but it sure gave me a lot more confidence in my safety when dealing with my fellow man.

Probably my closest encounter with death in the desert came one day when I was prospecting in the area of Yubay, north of Bahia. There is a lot of gold in the ground in that area. I have spent much of my time wandering those remote hills and canyons far from any road or house. In all the years that I have combed that area, I have yet to see it all, a testament to the vastness of the central Baja desert.

On this day, I had parked my truck in a dry sandy arroyo, beneath the almost sheer face of a cliff several hundred feet in elevation. I left the truck early in the morning, and began exploring an area on one end of the ridge that offered a convenient saddle that I could scale to get to the plateau above that was not reachable by truck. I was pleased to find several places that looked like they really might pay off with some more digging and sample analysis. I decided that I would spend the day working my way up to the top of the plateau so I could get the whole picture of what this particular part of the mountain might have to offer. I would then retrace my steps back to my truck. At some places, it was very difficult to climb from one level to another, but each time I did, I found interesting new sites to explore. I must admit that time got away from me that day, and by the time I got to the top of the mountain, I realized that there was no way I could make it all the way back down to my truck using the path I had taken up. I looked over the cliff, and could see my truck parked almost directly below. It was so enticingly close, only a few hundred yards down the sheer mountainside.

I weighed my options. It was summer, I had been sweating all day from my climb up the mountain, and had only a swallow or two of water left I could not really spend the night on top of the mountain. On the other hand, there was no way I could make it down the same way I had come before dark. But, traversing those steep cliffs in the dark would be foolhardy to say the least. I could see my truck below me, and calculated that it would take no more than a half an hour to reach it if I was able to descend from that side of the mountain. I contemplated the pros and cons of both alternatives, and then chose one. The wrong one! I looked carefully down one side of the ridge, a little way down from where I stood. I thought it might be a gentle enough slope to slide down on the seat of my pants. About a hundred feet below, the steep cliff flattened out into a little ridge, with some large rocks along the downhill edge. When I got there, I would be almost a third of the way down the mountain. It also looked like there was another ridge further down, but I could not tell for sure from where I stood on the top. I would have to scout it out a little more thoroughly when I got to the first ridge below. With a ridiculously unsubstantiated optimism, I walked resolutely to the edge of the cliff above the first ridge, sat down, and started my slide.

My plan was to slide down to a rock outcropping about 15 feet below me, and at that point to slow myself down by grabbing and holding onto it. Then I would head for a large agave plant that was growing out of a rock crevice below that, and work my way down the steep slope a little bit at a time. My bold plan was born out of my desire to reach my truck without having to backtrack all the way around the mountain. It was a bad plan, and things were about to begin to go seriously wrong, proving my decision even worse.

I pushed myself off the top, sliding on my butt down to the rock outcropping. My descent was a little faster than I thought, but I was still under control, and I grabbed the rock that was my goal exactly as I had intended. What I had NOT anticipated was that the rock would pull loose under my weight, which it did. I had intended to come to a complete stop, and then resume my downward journey under control. This was not the case however, as the rock only slowed me temporarily. I continued to slide down hill, picking up speed, soon completely out of control. Even worse, the rock I had loosened was bouncing down the hill just above me, and was plenty large enough to do serious damage if it hit me.

By the time I reached my original final target, the level ridge with the large boulders that would stop my downhill slide. I was traveling at an extremely high rate of speed. If I hit the rocks at this velocity, I would no doubt be injured. If I missed them, my momentum would carry me over the ridge and have me airborne over an almost vertical cliff. It would have meant a fall that would surely have killed me on the rocks at the canyon bottom. Things were happening so fast I was reacting only by instinct. I hit the ridge at a high rate of speed, and saw that I was going to hit the largest of the rocks head on. At the last second, I managed to put my hand out to cushion the blow. At that point, the rock that had been following me down the slide arrived. It had picked up speed fast on its downward journey. It crashed into the top of the boulder that had stopped my fall, not two feet above my head with a terrific bang. It bounced several feet into the air before tumbling in a spectacular fall to the valley floor. But I could not follow its flight, as the collision with the boulder had knocked me out cold.

I couldn't have been unconscious long, because when I came to rocks, pebbles, and sand were still finishing their slide all around me. My legs were almost covered with debris that I had dislodged during my fall. I was immediately aware of a terrific pain emanating from the arm I had used to fend off the collision with the boulder. It was a ghastly sight, lacerations so deep I could see bone beneath, and my entire hand and arm were covered with blood. I could not feel nor move my fingers, and using that hand or arm was impossible.

"Ok Herman," I thought, "you *pinche gringo*, you have really gotten yourself in a pickle this time. Were you just too lazy to go back the long way? Have you forgotten the prudence and care that you had always used when alone in the desert? I don't want to be here. I don't want to face the dangers I have brought on myself by my own miscalculations. I would much rather be having an evening *cerveza* with the boys back in Bahia. Well, no sense in berating yourself now Herman. Better save all your energy and creativity to find a way out of this situation."

I forced myself to calm down, and take stock of my situation, which was not good. I was stuck on a narrow ridge, less than half way down the face of the cliff, still at least 200 feet above my truck. One arm was useless, and I was losing blood fast. Going back up the slope was not an option, it was far too steep. I could either stay where I was, or continue on down. Staying put to wait for help was not an astute choice, as I was many miles from the closest rancho, on a seldom used road that might not see two vehicles a month, and would doubtless have bled to death long before anyone chanced to happened by. Not only was I losing blood, but I had been sweating in the hot sun all day, and had depleted my system of vital salts by replacing the sweat with pure water. This depletion would be exacerbated by the loss of blood, and I knew that severe muscle cramps would be the first symptoms. In my situation, such cramps could prove fatal.

As quickly and as calmly as I could under the circumstances, I weighed all the factors involved, and concluded that my best chance for survival was to try to get down safely to the truck. I simply could not stay where I was. Under normal circumstances no one in his right mind would attempt to descend that almost sheer cliff, but I did not have the luxury of being in normal circumstances. Attempting the descent was probable death, but remaining where I was with the loss of blood I was experiencing was almost certain death. I chose probable over certain.

I must say that at that point, when I had become determined to continue going down, I felt a calming acceptance of my decision, and a commitment to carrying it out to the best of my ability. Whatever was going to happen would happen. All that was left to me was to do the best that I could, and I resolved to do just that. I tore my shirt into strips of clothe which I tied as tightly as I could around my wounds to stem the flow of blood. This left me with only my undershirt for protection, but I had little choice in the matter. I then studied the cliff below very carefully. Obviously it was foolhardy to try a descent here, but I had to do it. The only positive I could see was that a little to my left, the slope while not much less steep, was dotted with bushes and shrubs growing out of the near vertical rock face. I decided to try to go from plant to plant, holding onto them for what I fervently hoped would be a slow and controlled descent onto the valley floor, and the safety of my truck.

Working with only one hand, I started carefully down the face of the cliff, this time on my stomach. I found to my joy that I had two very positive things going for me. Firstly, the cliff was pure rock, and covered with crevices and chinks that I could use for foot and handholds. Secondly, there were more bushes growing out of the cracks in the rock on this part of the cliff, and the roots were very firmly fixed. I tested each one by pulling hard on it while still maintaining a secure hold elsewhere, before having to depend on it for my next move. Without exception they held firm and could support my entire weight.

Using the utmost care to maintain firm foot and hand holds, I descended from bush to bush down the cliff and within an hour, had made downward progress of over 100 feet. I was now the equivalent of only ten stories above the rocks on the canyon floor. As the afternoon wore on into evening, I calculated that if I could keep up this rate of progress, I would reach the valley floor by nightfall. With every move I was getting lower, and closer to my goal.

"Damn Herman! Don't tell me you are going to get out of THIS one!"

I made all the usual deals with God that a person does at times of crisis like this. "Just get me out of this one, big guy, and I will never have to ask you for help again, I promise!"

The lower I got, the more I began to gain confidence. I was a little worried because I was beginning also to experience brief periods of dizziness, which I attributed to loss of blood. Every ten feet I was able to traverse increased my chances of survival, even if I did fall. Indeed I found myself at no more than thirty five feet of height when my luck came to an end. I selected a bush growing out of the rock two feet below my top hand hold, and gave it a test pull, as I had done a hundred times on my descent. It held fast, so I left my foothold and used the bush to hold my weight as I probed for a secure foothold below. I guess I had changed the angle at which I was pulling on the trunk of the bush too much. The roots held fast, but the trunk broke off just above my hand before I had a firm foothold. For a moment I teetered there, desperately trying to keep my balance, but could not. I dug both of the toes of my boots into the cliff hoping to find a solid foothold, but they both just slid down a sheer face. I only remember a thought flashing through my mind that I had done my best, and I was ready to accept my fate. I was just too tired to fight any longer, and lost consciousness.

I awoke, and found that I had indeed made it to the bottom, the hard way. But surprisingly I was still alive. I must have been unconscious for quite a while, because it was pitch dark. My hand and arm throbbed with an agonizing pain, and I had added a nasty gash to my forehead, and a hundred more cuts and scrapes on my legs, back, and stomach. In short, I was a mess. I looked around me, and there, not two hundred yards away, in the moonlight I could see my truck! I was unsure if I could stand or not, so very slowly, I tested my legs, and found I could indeed stand, in spite of a myriad of cuts and bruises and strained muscles. After taking only a few steps toward the truck, however, I was hit with a sharp pain in the muscle of my upper leg which caused me to buckle to the ground. Cramps! The depletion of salts and the loss of blood were taking their toll. Before I could attempt to rise again, the other leg cramped up, even worse than the first. My truck and safety was only a short distance away, but I could no longer walk.

I had come through so much, and was so close to survival, that I was filled with a determination to get to that truck any way I could. I could visualize the next vehicle through the canyon finding my truck, and my dead body lying close to it. That was NOT going to happen! I literally had to crawl to cover the short distance to the pickup. It took a long time, but I made it. I pulled myself up by the door handle, and by hanging onto the truck, was able to stand erect. I reached for a plastic gallon bottle of water in the bed, and took a very long and wonderful drink, immediately followed by a healthy dose of the salts my body needed. I always took a jar of these salts to the desert with me, and that habit now helped save my life.

Using materials from the truck, I redid all my bandages, and was glad to see that most of the bleeding had been stemmed. Only the deep gashes on my hand and wrist continued to produce bright red blood, and I bound these areas with new bandages and tied them as tightly as I could. Driving at night was out of the question, so I crawled onto the front seat of the pickup and spent a fitful night drifting into and out of sleep. With the first rays of the morning sun, I started for home.

I knew I had a three hour drive to get to Bahia, and I was not yet out of danger. The salts and the water had helped immensely, but I had lost a lot of blood. I also had only one arm with which I could drive, and my old workhorse pickup was a bear to steer even using both hands. I proceeded down the canyons and ravines toward the main road for about an hour and a half, going very slowly so as not to get stuck in the patches of loose sand. I had come too far to allow myself to die that way. The steering wheel of the truck began to pull ever more sharply toward the left, and I had to hold it very tightly to maintain a course straight ahead. At last it became almost impossible to steer, so I stopped the truck and got out. The front tire on the driver's side had a large cactus spine protruding from the sidewall, and the tire was completely flat. Oh God! What else can happen? I knew that I was only a couple of miles from the main road to Bahia, and briefly considered driving that distance on the flat. Surely on that road some one would come along and fix the tire for me. No, I decided that with the flat, there was just too much chance of getting bogged down in the sand, and that would put me in an even worse situation than I already was facing. It would be easier, and wiser, to just change the tire. I had the spare, and all the tools, but I was just not sure that I had the energy left to do the job by myself. All I knew for certain was that I had to try.

I got out the lug wrench and the jack and began to change the tire. The morning was getting very warm, and by the time I got the truck jacked up, I was sweating profusely, out of energy, and beginning to accept the idea that I would just have to give up. The shade under the truck was so cool, calming, and wonderful, for a while I just lay there, feeling strangely comfortable, accepting my fate with no regrets. I started drifting into a very welcome sleep. Suddenly, on a *maguey* plant not twenty feet from me, two ravens got into a disagreement. Their screeching and beating of wings jolted me from my drowsiness, and my head cleared. Summoning up all my remaining energy, I managed to finish changing the tire. Within ten minutes, I had reached the main road, but there was no traffic in sight, so I decided to drive the rest of the way to town. It was not a good idea, the loss of blood was making me woozy, and I was drifting perilously close to losing consciousness. I made it all the way to town though, and drove right up to the tiny medical clinic close to the Plaza. As I brought my truck to a stop in front of the clinic, it all caught up to me, and I again passed out. My truck rolled slowly forward, and hit the big Mesquite tree that still stands in front of the clinic. By luck, I slumped forward over the wheel, and in doing so, activated the horn. At least, that is what they told me. When I awoke again, I was in a cool, clean clinic bed with fresh bandages on my arm, and an IV giving me a transfusion.

It was several months before I again was able to go back into the desert in my quest for gold. I had left my favorite rock hammer at the base of the cliff, and I wanted to see if it was still there. I went with a friend and actually did find my hammer.

"Hey Herman, where did you actually come down?" Pablo asked?

"Right here," I said.

He looked up at the sheer face of the cliff. "No, seriously, where was it?"

"Just above us," I insisted.

"Come on, don't bullshit me."

I never could convince him, or anyone else, that I came down that sheer rock face and lived to tell about it. The experience had been good for me in a way, as I became much more realistic in my appraisal of what I could, and could not do when alone in the desert. I must admit I haven't really been successful in keeping all those deals I made with God for His help in getting me out of there. I hope I never have to ask again, because the next time he might not believe me.

CHAPTER 13

Los Rancheros

*I*t would have been much more difficult, if not impossible, for me to have spent as much time as I did prospecting the central Baja desert, had it not been for the existence of the Rancheros who lived there. This hardy breed of man helped me in so many ways, and I have always been grateful to them for their assistance. In addition to being in their debt, I also hold them in very high esteem for the skills they have mastered in not only making a living from the desert, but carving out lives that are in many ways as rich and rewarding as others I have seen in far more fertile lands.

When the Jesuits came to Adac, as the Cochimi had named the area, and founded the mision San Borja many years ago, the surrounding land supported a larger population of Indians than any of the older missions further south could boast. At its height, the number of souls being saved by the Catholics numbered over three thousand. Unfortunately, as is well known, the good Padres displayed more skill at saving souls than saving lives, and the population steadily dwindled until these remarkable natives disappeared altogether.

In the beginning, there was no way that the immediate mission area could support that number of mouths. The Cochimi had been nomadic, and had followed a yearly route that had included the seasonal sources of food available in the area. The good fathers wanted that to cease. The Indians would stay in one place, do the work they had been assigned, and learn the ways of civilization. In order to feed everyone, it was necessary to build little settlements around all the sources of water within one or two days walk of the mission. The mission itself would host as many Indians as possible at any given time, but these smaller peripheral "Visitas" fed the majority. The Indians would be shifted around on a regular basis so that each individual got a period of time at the mission itself. San Borja was able to feed a greater number of Indians because of the food that was raised on these visitas and sent to the mission.

This arrangement worked very well for the Jesuits for a number of decades. The visitas had buildings, fertile fields, systems of irrigation, and in time groves of fruit trees, vineyards, and a number of different types of grain crops. They also raised several kinds of domestic animals. There was plenty of food for both animals and people alike. The only flaw in the system was that due to low birth rates and high death rates, the mission was steadily saving more souls, only to soon send them winging to Heaven. The number of live Indians decreased at an alarming rate. A people once free to roam, but now captive, having had a diet that the land dictated, but now largely European, that was used to living in small family groups, but now forced to live among hundreds, did not fare well. Their souls might have been saved, but their spirits were broken. All too soon, the visitas were no longer necessary to sustain the whole population, and all the remaining Indians could be housed on the mission grounds. Most of the visitas were abandoned, and fell into ruin.

With the expulsion of the Jesuits, things changed rapidly in Baja. The Jesuits had resisted all efforts on the part of the Crown in Madrid to secularize the peninsula. With the coming of the Franciscans, all that changed. Galvez, the envoy from Spain, encouraged settlement by non-religious in central Baja. He also granted lands to the few remaining Indians, and tried to encourage them to farm for a living. The Cochimi had no concept of the ownership of land however, and almost without exception sold their land quickly and cheaply to any takers. Many of the previously abandoned visitas were taken over by the lay population that did exist, and new immigrants from mainland Mexico and Europe. The dilapidated buildings were restored, the ground tilled, and animals brought in. Irrigation networks were repaired, and water flowed into the fields once again. The visitas had become the Ranchos.

This hardy stock of Rancheros that had its beginnings in the early decades of the nineteenth century was the wellspring of the people that I met and got to know in my wanderings around San Borja Adac. They were termed, and are still called to this day, "Los Rancheros." Much of what I know about getting along in the deserts of Baja I have learned from these people.

The average ranchero knows almost as much about the desert, its plants and animals, its moods, its dangers and rewards as did the Cochimi before them. A lot of the technical knowledge of survival in the desert was handed down from the Indians to the ranchers, and from the ranchers to me.

My trips into the desert would often take me through these oases of green and pastures of plenty that dotted the dry desert. I got into the habit of always taking with me several boxes of .22 long rifle bullets. Almost every rancho had at least one .22 rifle, and ammunition was hard to come by. I never sold the bullets, rather always used them as a gift. Believe me, I got more than their worth in return! As time went on, I struck up first relationships and later even friendships with these proud people. There was a certain sameness to the ranchos. They always had water, a dependable year-round source. There was fertile soil nearby, and crops were grown. Inevitably there were fruit trees, vegetable and herb gardens, root crops and vineyards. The places were usually busy with all sorts of animals. Few needed to be penned, as they were dependent on the water supply the rancho afforded, and there was really no other place nearby to go. There were chickens, goats, burros, and horses. Every rancho had cattle, some only a few for milk, others many for yearly sales.

In the early days, few children left the ranchos before adulthood. They did not go to school at all, but developed the skills they needed on the ranch. As time went on, more and more went to live with their relatives in nearby towns with schools, such as Bahia de los Angeles, Guerrero Negro, or even as far away as La Paz or Ensenada. More and more of these sons and daughters chose not to return to the ranchos, preferring the more modern lifestyles afforded by larger populations.

The mission at San Borja was abandoned by the Dominicans in 1818, because there were no more Cochimi left. The Catholic church continued to send Priests on special occasions however, and the local rancheros could have their children baptized, or hold marriages and funerals when needed. These marriages usually sprung from pairings between ranch families, and few outsiders joined the somewhat closed society. Most modern day ranchero families can trace their origins back to the 1800's.

Health care was about on a par with the Indian days when I arrived. Every rancho had its own family graveyard. Anyone severely injured or ill usually joined it in short order. Other than the still existing Jesuit roads, there were only footpaths through the desert, and horses or burros for transportation. Today, most if not all ranchos have trucks, and passable dirt roads connect the ranches with the few roads that lead to towns. But in the early days, they seldom ventured too far from the rancho. There was much work to do, and their needs for dealing with the outside world were few. In addition, in those days there were men who would pack up a burro chain with supplies for the ranchos. Since the rancheros had little money, they would trade the goods from town for things the rancho could produce, such as firewood, cheese, fruit, soap, hides, and last but not least – gold!

When I first arrived in the San Borja region, the amount of gold these ranchos produced was very small. The two main reasons for this were that the traders from town that the rancheros had been trading the gold with did not give them a fair rate. The trader, not the rancher, made most of the profit on the gold when it was sold in town. This diminished the incentive to spend time on the difficult work of locating and processing the ore. Secondly, the methods they were using had not changed much for generations. They recovered only a small percentage of the gold the ore actually held.

I did what I could to make their little cottage industry mining projects more efficient. By far the most helpful thing I could do was to show them how to be more effective at getting the gold out of the ore. I taught them to use mercury to recover the gold particles too small to be seen by the human eye. That alone doubled the amount of gold they were able to get from the ore. I showed them different ways to choose the best places to get their ore samples, which also resulted in an increased yield of gold.

Finally, and most importantly, I gave them a much fairer price for their gold than the traders had been giving them, and paid them in cash. As time went on, the rancheros made more and more frequent trips to town in their ancient pickup trucks, so they had more use for cash. They took in their farm goods, sold them themselves, and paid pesos in town for the things they needed. The pack burro traders all but disappeared.

Because of all these things, I was able to establish and maintain an excellent rapport with these ranch families, many of which I still enjoy. This would serve me very well, as being able to trade with them made my trips into the hills much more comfortable. I could obtain fresh vegetables and fruit when I needed any. I also borrowed the use of their burros on occasion to help pack in my equipment. Best of all, I made, and enjoyed for years, a nice little side business of buying and selling their gold.

Sierra San Borja

CHAPTER 14

$\mathcal{E}$arly in my search for Baja gold I lived at the starkly beautiful and remote site of the Mision San Borja Adac. I loved the place. It had ample water, supplied by year-round spring, and the soil is amazingly fertile. A wide variety of crops can be grown there as long as they are watered adequately. I remember a huge Mango tree that grew near one water hole, I have never seen a bigger one in my life. It was a prolific bearer of fruit, and I passed many an afternoon siesta in its ample shade. Adac had a lot of charm, it had a lot of beauty, a lot of serenity and peace, but mostly I liked it because it also had a lot of gold! I would use the mission as a base for my prospecting, and from there could range far and wide in the surrounding hills.

Even though the Jesuits and their Indian workers had beaten me to a lot of the gold, there was still more than enough to support a single miner who would be satisfied with a few grams a day. There was very little water outside of the oasis itself, but there were a few ranches here and there in the hills and valleys nearby. I would often drop by these ranches for water, or to trade for some fresh food, especially if I had been away from my house for a while. I wandered the Sierra San Borja and the Sierra San Pedro to the south of the mission. Even further south were Pico Echeverria and Pico Maximilliano, both volcanic peaks renamed since colonial times, and likely spots to find gold. Both peaks could be reached by rough roads through the desert, at some points roads that had been originally constructed by the Jesuits two hundred years before.

As I have explained, early on in my Baja roaming, when I went into the desert, I was actually searching for gold on three separate levels. First, I was looking for the small specs of gold hidden among the desert sand, and even some nuggets, that had been worn from the original vein deposits. Secondly, I was seeking these veins themselves. And last, but not least, I was searching for the lost Jesuit treasure. I found two out of three, not a bad average I guess!

With these three goals in mind, I spent a great deal of time in the hills around San Borja, probably as much as any Gringo ever has. I got to know the area very well, and discovered abundant evidence that the area, especially close to the springs, had been used heavily by the Indians. I have found a number of Cochimi points in the area, rather skillfully made arrowheads, usually small. Some larger ones were used for bigger game, or for the most dangerous game of all – other Cochimi! For many animals, the Indians preferred to use only the wooden arrow shafts themselves, with points hardened by fire, and no stone arrowhead at all.

One type of artifact that I have found several times is a mystery to me. It is a round clay disk, about the size and shape of a half dollar with two small holes bored through near the center. I do not know what they were used for, but thought maybe they were used to hold drawstrings of the nets they used to carry objects as they moved through the desert. They almost certainly came from far to the north, or from the mainland, as the Indians of Baja were not known to work with clay.

The desert around San Borja is fairly typical of all of central Baja. Probably the most prolific native trees are two closely related species, the ocotillo and the Palo Adan. It takes a while to tell them apart, but once you know what to look for, it becomes possible to do so reliably in almost every instance. This is one of the few places that the habitat of the two overlaps, and both are found in abundance. When dead and dried, both look like hollow tubes, with a latticework of holes. One often sees them used for bird perches, for which use they are ideal. In general, ocotillo is straight branches springing from the ground in a group, with branching only near the tips. The palo adan has a short, thick trunk, ending only a few inches above the ground, and each branch has more bifurcations and many smaller branches. They both have vivid red flowers in the spring.

One other tree to be very aware of if you hazard into the desert regions on foot is the elephant tree. You have seen them from the road if you have traveled through this part of Baja. They have white, bulbous trunks, and branches that extend only a few inches before being greatly reduced in circumference and ending in a small patch of leaves. "Elephant tree" is really one name given to a variety of species that look alike. This is one tree I would like to warn you about. The Cochimi Indians called these trees the "Arbol de Pletcha", which means the "Tree of Arrows". When I first heard this, it was very puzzling to me, because if there was ever a tree that would NOT produce good arrows, it was this one. Its branches are short and rounded, absolutely impossible to fashion arrows from. I later learned that this is not at all what the name implies. The Indians learned the hard way that if one sleeps under this type of tree, it sheds tiny, arrow shaped nettles during the night. These look for all the world like little arrows, and if enough of them get into your eyes, they can cause blindness. Every Indian knew to avoid the "Tree of Arrows."

Most of my mining in the San Borja area was dry mining for placer gold. For that purpose my main tool was my dry washer. Using this wonderful invention, and finding a few nuggets by sight, I was able to eke out a few grams of gold most days. Sometimes less, sometimes more, but always enough to satisfy me, and my needs, and as time went by I got better at it. I never did find that big vein or lode from which all the little flecks came, I suppose a lot of them have been found before me, or completely eroded away. I am equally sure that some still remain, hidden in the earth. I couldn't find them, but perhaps some one who follows my path in life will. I wish him good luck!

In addition to gold, the Baja is rich in other types of precious and semi-precious stones. One of the most common types found here are those in the quartz family. As you drive the roads of Baja, you have no doubt seen the seams of quarts exposed on the roadside cuts, or on hillsides laid bare by erosion. Quartz is a very hard stone, too brittle for use as tools, but with a very pleasant glassy texture. The whole family is composed primarily of silicon dioxide, (SiO_2), but comes in many forms. The most common forms of quartz are the milky, smoky, and rose colors. This family also includes chalcedony and Jasper. Some are used extensively in jewelry making, such as the agate, amethyst, agate and opal. Opals and agates have varieties called fire opal or fire agate, which flash color as they are moved in the light.

An interesting form of this crystalline structure is the geode. I am sure you have seen these at jewelry stores, or on countertop displays of many kinds. They are basically rounded stones, very ordinary looking on the outside, but hiding inside a hollow crystal packed center of unbelievable beauty. They are usually displayed cut in half with a rock saw. These are normally found as small round stones, but once you have seen a few, you can pretty well identify them from among all similar small stones that do not contain crystals. I find them routinely during my prospecting trips, and although they are interesting, I ignore them. They are just too heavy, and I am after bigger game, that wonderful yellow metal called gold.

In recent years, as my trips seeking gold lessened in frequency, I began taking groups of people, usually visiting Americans to gather these pretty semi-precious gems in the mountains around Bahia de los Angeles. I really enjoy these trips, as I love to see the enthusiasm and joy with which each new find is greeted. It has enabled me to meet and become friends with a wide variety of people from not only the United States, but from throughout the world. Many of them come back time and again, and often come and visit my little house by the beach. I guess the bottom line is that I enjoy seeing in them when they find an agate, the same feeling I get when finding a good sized nugget. The same feeling, but mine is worth a lot more! Now, if only each of these people would buy just one copy of my book.........I'd be rich!

After a few years exploring the region using San Borja as a base, I decided to move to a spot on the beach at Bahia de los Angeles, and I have lived there ever since. I still went out into the hills south and East of San Borja on occasion, but my focus for finding gold was pretty much permanently shifted to the north. When I left San Borja, I left a bit of my heart behind. It was a good part of my life, and is a remarkable place when you get to know it well. If you have visited it, you will know what I mean. If you have not, do so at your first opportunity.

Chicken, Beans and Rice

CHAPTER 15

It was one of those patently beautiful mornings that Bahia de los Angeles is blessed with so frequently. The sun had risen over the islands offshore on a warm and sunny October day, with it's usual light show of oranges and reds and purples. Like most of my neighbors, I tend to go to sleep soon after the sun sets, and get up before it rises again to begin it's next trip across the sky.

By about eleven o'clock, my breakfast was beginning to fade, and I decided to go get some lunch at my favorite place on the beach, the Villa Bahia. I drove the four kilometers out on the road to La Gringa, and was delighted to find that the cook, Lupita, had already begun preparing lunch for a group of guests. Be it lunch, or breakfast or dinner, Lupita always had enough for one more person, and I think I was her favorite pest. I have found that in life, it is always a good idea to be nice to some one who can really cook, and I knew I was always welcome in her kitchen.

I went out and sat at an outdoor table by the beach, shaded by a palm frond palapa, and was enjoying the pleasant morning breeze that had sprung up when Lupita came out with my lunch. She had made a dish of chicken, and beans, and rice. The smell of that food triggered a memory that I had carried with me for many years. As I ate, and watched a good sized pod of dolphins pass offshore, my mind wandered back, to a war, a jungle, and a wonderful group of people that I sincerely hoped were alive had prospered over the years.

The same bright sun was shining those many years ago on Luzon Island in the Philippines. I was taking my turn as lookout. I stood up to take another look, and as I focused my binoculars, I saw what I had expected, but hoped not to see. On the opposite side of the valley, far below me six Japanese tanks were advancing toward my position. They were spread out in a line, side by side, and behind them were several hundred Japanese soldiers, on foot.

"Ok," I thought, "There they are. Time to get the hell out of here!"

I ran to my parked jeep, and sped back about 8 kilometers to the village I had been staying at for a week. As I pulled into the grassy area in the center of the group of huts, and skidded the jeep to a halt, I yelled to the two uniformed men that waited there. "Time to haul ass – let's go!"

Then, on a whim, I decided to deny the Japs the use of the jeep. I opened the hood, took off the distributor cap, took out the rotor and hurled it far into the jungle where it would never be found.

For days we had been waiting, and preparing for this moment. Our orders were to evacuate the entire village, and head through the jungle to a point on the coast where the natives would be relocated safely to the south. There were three of us, myself, a Navy Boatswain's mate First Class, a Torpedoman First, and an Australian soldier who had been a coast watcher and radioman. The plan we had devised was that we would split up the villagers into three groups, and each lead one would go by a different route. We reasoned that it would be more difficult for the Japanese to follow three groups, and that at least some of us would have a better chance to escape. We knew very well what lay in store for us should the Japs catch up to us.

Things went smoothly, as we had prepared and rehearsed many times for that moment. In only a few minutes, our groups had been formed, each person had an assigned load to carry, and we were heading out of the village into the jungle. My group consisted of me, a Filipino guerrilla guide, and sixteen women and children. There were no men in any of the three groups. They had all left the village long ago to join groups of resistance fighters that harassed the approaching army in whatever way they could. That was the primary reason for evacuating the village. The Japanese would have dealt very harshly with them, for they would know where the men must be. Neither my Filipino guide nor I took a rifle. That would be too heavy to carry through the jungle for the distance we had to go, and should we meet the Japanese, resistance would in any case be futile. We did each have side arms, which we would use only in an emergency, since silence was absolutely essential to our survival.

Food made up the bulk of what we took with us. We would need to keep up our strength if we were to make it. We could rely upon finding sources of water in the jungle. Food for that many people was another matter. The villagers all understood, and had taken only that which was the most important to our journey. I was very happy with the progress my group made on the first day, and felt if we could avoid getting lost, or having to slow down for any reason, we could beat the Japs to the coast. By the time we stopped for the day, we were a good fifteen kilometers from the village, every step of the way through thick jungle. The Filipino ladies began cooking a meal, over a very small fire, and with materials that produced little smoke. We were all very hungry after several hours of walking, and I can still remember the wonderful aroma that arose from that cooking pot! They were making the most wonderful dish I have ever tasted – Chicken, beans, and rice. Mine was served on a broad leaf with a spoon improvised from bamboo, but it might as well have been on Spode China with a spoon of solid silver, as wonderful as that meal was. To this day, I have never tasted anything better. They offered me seconds, and I had to summon up all my will to decline the offer, as I was not sure there would be enough for all the women, who ate last. I went to sleep that night thankful for both that meal, and the distance between us and the Japanese.

As the days of trekking through the jungle passed, we continued to make good time. All was going well, we had had no injuries or accidents, our spirits were high, and we were staying ahead of our pursuers. I am not sure, but I suspect that once or twice our Filipino guide was a bit lost, but always got us back on track again. The only thing that concerned me was that the food was running out, and I had no idea how many more days it would take to reach our destination. After the first few days, we had only lard and bread left, yet those remarkable women made even that taste palatable. They toasted the bread, and heated the lard. We dipped the bread into the lard, and believe it or not, as hungry as we all were, it was palatable and we looked forward to it. The women saw to it that the men and children always ate first and had as much as they could spare with the rationing that was necessary. They cut their own portions to the greatest extent they could. May God bless those women, wherever they may be today.

After a few days of nothing but bread and lard, we got a lucky break. The kids found some nests that wild chickens had made, and each had several eggs in it! They gleefully brought them in to our camp one evening, hoping for a special treat of boiled eggs. The only problem was that we didn't have a pot to boil them in. I guess I had been in the jungle long enough to go partly native, so I devised our own cooking pot on the spot. I cut a section near the bottom of a giant bamboo stalk, left the thick bottom intact, and cut off the top making a good sized receptacle of it. We filled it partially with water, and put the eggs in it. Then we placed the bamboo section over the fire. I reasoned that the fire would be able to boil the water in the bamboo before it burned through the bottom, and I was right! Soon the water was boiling, and the eggs were ready to eat. The kids who had found the eggs claimed theirs first, grabbing them right out of the water. I will never know how they did that without getting their fingers burned, but they did. We had enough eggs so that everyone in our party had one, and the kids felt very proud of themselves.

One wonderful morning, the guide led us onto a road through the jungle. This was something he never had done before on our march, and I guessed that we must be very near the village for him to take such a risk. I was right, and after about an hour on that road, I saw ahead the most beautiful blue water I have ever seen! We came to a white sand beach, and a few hundred yards down to our left were a group of huts. There were several native boats riding at anchor just offshore. As we approached the village, the Australian ran up to me and pumped my hand vigorously. His group had arrived safely only the day before. He was obviously delighted to see that we had made it, and I will never forget his sincere greeting. He told me that Navy reconnaissance had reported that the Japanese were still over 50 kilometers away, and advancing slowly. We now only had to wait for the third group to arrive, and we would all be taken to safety far behind the American lines.

As we entered the village, I saw what looked to me like giant spiders hung up on bamboo drying racks. Damn those things looked ugly! To make matters worse, for our first meal in the village, they tried to serve me some of that hideous stuff. I of course refused, as hungry as I was, and to this day will not knowingly eat octopus!

Two days later, the third party arrived at the village. We had all made it in good shape, not a person was injured or lost on the way. The Australian broke radio silence for the first time, and sent a coded message. Within hours, we saw a US Navy ship appear offshore, and small boats were sent in to evacuate us. Soon I was back into my old world of shipboard life, the heat and damp and noises of the jungle faded into a memory. I will always remember that Australian fellow. I wish I had gotten his name. Those wonderful brave and gentle women, the open and exuberant children, will serve as a pleasant memory always. I remember each one of them.

The Legendary Sleeping Jailbreak of Bahia de los Angeles

$\mathscr{M}$anuel Flores was the Delegado of the little town of Bahia de los Angeles. He was a very good choice for the job. The job of the Delegado was a combination of mayor, police chief, fire chief, and in short, represented in one person the total local authority for the pueblo. Manuel was a good worker, and took his position very seriously. He did everything by the book, followed orders well, and was as reliable person there was in the town. True, he did not have much imagination, or creativity, but he did not really need them. The job demanded steady, unwavering adherence to rules, and for that, he was perfectly suited. Manuel Flores was the last person one could imagine who would aid and abet a jailbreak, but that is what he did.

It all began when Guadalupe Flores, Manuel's wife, complained about all the boats that Manuel had collected as part of his duties, and had stored in his yard. If some one was caught fishing without a license, his boat was confiscated until a hefty fine was paid. Often it would take the owner considerable time to collect the necessary money, and the boat stayed in Manuel's yard until the fine was paid. Also, since Bahia de los Angeles was an active stop along the transfer route for illegal drugs heading north, boats were from time to time found abandoned, or seized in hot pursuit on the gulf. If fines were not paid, or boats not claimed, the normal procedure was for them to be confiscated by the Federal police from the office in Ensenada, and sold at auction. That was the normal procedure. But, in the Baja, nothing is quite worthy of the term 'normal'. Many months, even years, would go by before some one from the Federal government came for the unclaimed boats, and even then, not all of them made it to the auction block.

Guadalupe Flores usually respected the wishes of her husband, but as the number of boats in the yard grew, she put her foot down, and told Manuel "The boats have to go. Soon we will not have room to even walk in our yard. Get rid of the boats!"

Manuel knew that when Lupe felt that strongly about some issue, it was best to just go along with her or there would be no peace and quiet around the house. He decided to ask Jesus Arce if he could leave the boats at his house. Jesus was a good choice, as he lived alone in a small ramshackle house on the far edge of town, and had much unused space around him.

Jesus agreed to store the boats, but asked Manuel "What if some one comes in the night and steals them?"

Manuel assured him that he would not be responsible, and he would handle any problems along that line if they came up.

The agreement was sealed with a handshake, and the impounded boats were transferred one by one to an open space behind Jesus' house. Guadalupe Flores was happy again. She had the use of her yard back, and this made life once more tranquil for Manuel. Every time a boat was confiscated, it was taken to Jesus' house to be stored. This worked out very well for everyone involved, and much time passed before any problem arose. One day, however, Manuel was hauling a boat to park with the others, when it occurred to him that even though he had been bringing boats on a regular basis, the collection did not seem to be growing larger.

Becoming a little suspicious, Manuel returned to his office for a list of the boats he had taken to storage. Manuel was a methodical man, and kept such records and reports faithfully. Sure enough, when he compared his list to the boats in the yard, several were missing. Manuel confronted Jesus with the inescapable evidence of the loss of the boats. Jesus could not understand the importance of the matter. "But Manuel, I get no rent for storing the boats, what am I to do? I have to eat too, just like you, and besides, these boats are abandoned, and not doing anyone any good while they sit here on the land, and there are many fish in the gulf." The two men had a widely divergent view of how the law worked. Jesus applied logic and common sense, Manuel applied discipline, control, and unquestioning adherence to authority. Jesus admitted he had been selling the boats, but insisted he had sold them for very little money, just enough to cover his "rent" for storage, and to sometimes buy him tortillas and beans for his suppers. At this point, Manuel was aware that he had a very large problem if and when the Federales ever came to claim their boats.

Fate can be very cruel, and it was only a few days later that he received orders from Ensenada to have the boats ready for inventory the following week. It began a very troubled week for Manuel. He was at a loss to find any reasonable solution to his problem. All he could do was wait for the other shoe to fall, which it soon did. Two government cars and a pickup truck arrived at the office of the Delegado, which faced the town plaza. Several very impressive men, extremely official in their spotless uniforms with shiny buttons and badges entered his office. They requested to see the impound yard, and Manuel, as though taking the final march of a condemned man, led them to Jesus' yard. In a matter of seconds the discrepancy was discovered. Manuel professed complete ignorance of the possible cause of the disappearance, and Jesus was summoned from his house. He seemed as confused and like Manuel, at a loss for an explanation.

"I do not know, Senores, the boats must have been stolen."

"Stolen?" the Federale in charge bellowed. "Then why did you not report this to the Delegado?"

Jesus scratched his head pensively, "I do not know Senor, it must have just happened last night!"

The Federale turned purple with rage at this nonsense, and turned on his heel and left with his entourage. They drove to the beach where the pangas were tied, and list in hand, began examining each boat. They soon identified several that were on the list, and returned to Manuel's office. Manuel was ordered to bring in Jesus immediately, and it did not take much interrogation to persuade him to confess to selling the boats. Manuel was shaking with fear, waiting to see what the Capitan of the Federales would do. It could well cost him his job and a lot more, if they decided to be nasty about it. Jesus was in deep trouble too, but had much less to lose. He had no job, no money, and no possessions worth seizing.

The head Federale was quiet for several seconds, mulling the situation and forming his response.

At last he said "Arce, you are going to prison." Jesus blanched and his heart froze. "We have located only a few of the missing boats. Where are the others?"

Jesus croaked in a weak voice "I do not know Senor, other villages I guess." His voice trailed off, and for the first time he felt really guilty of a crime. The Federale turned to Manuel.

"Flores. You are to immediately place this man under arrest and put him in your jail until we can send him to Ensenada. . The extremely bad judgment you have displayed in this matter will be reported, and a decision will be made soon. You are to begin immediately to recover all the boats we have found here, and as many of the others as you can find in other nearby villages or fishing camps." The entire contingent then returned to their vehicles and left the village. Manuel put Jesus in one of the two cells in the tiny town jail, and set about recovering the misappropriated boats. He wondered how he had let himself get into this predicament, and hoped things would get better. They didn't.

On his first night in the jail, Jesus created yet another crisis, this time not only for Manuel, but for a lot of the people in town who lived near the jail. You see, Jesus snored. And it was not your ordinary, irritating snore. It was of legendary proportions. Once asleep, he emitted a steady succession of low pitched, foghorn loud snores. Each one lasted about ten seconds, followed by a short pause, and then another, and another, and another. Everything within a 40 yard radius seemed to vibrate at the same pitch as each snore. To make matters worse, at random intervals, the smooth succession of snores was punctuated by a loud snort. After each snort, there was a varying interval of silence, and then inevitably the resumption of the snores.

Manuel and Guadalupe's house was adjacent to the jail, and as it was summertime, all windows were left open. The first night they both sat bolt upright with the first series of nasal blasts emanating from the jail. They listened carefully, trying to identify the source of the sound. No, it was not the thunder of some storm far out in the gulf. It was not the blow of a whale close to the shore, but what could it be? Roosters who normally waited dutifully for the dawn to crow, started in with their cries. Dogs began to bark and howl in a cacophony of sound. Manuel arose quickly, dressed and went to the jail to see what was happening. Once in the room, the sound became several decibels higher, and he felt the wooden floor vibrating under his boots.

Juan Torres, who occupied the other cell due to a regrettable bout of tequila binges, was standing with both hands gripping the bars between the cells glaring at Jesus.

"Stop him!" he yelled to Manuel. "Please stop him!" Manuel went to the cell door and shook it loudly. The snoring continued.

He shouted "Jesus!" at the top of his lungs.

"It is no use Manuel", Juan said. "I have been shouting at him for ten minutes but he will not wake up."

Manuel opened the cell door and shook Jesus vigorously.

Finally, mercifully, the snoring stopped. Jesus looked up at Manuel questioningly. "What is wrong Manuel?"

"You are snoring Jesus, very loudly!"

Jesus saddened, and rubbed his eyes. "Yes, I know. That is why both of my wives have left me. It is also why I live alone at the edge of town. I am sorry my friend, I have been this way all my life."

"Well, you will just have to stop it!", Manuel said with more hope than logic.

"But I cannot, because when I am asleep, I do not know that I am snoring."

"Well, you will just have to stay awake then." was Manuel's solution.

"I will try." Jesus promised.

Manuel went back to bed. He and Guadalupe lay in bed for some minutes, enjoying the wonderful silence. Both had started to drift off to sleep when it started again. The snores, the snorts, the vibration. These were followed shortly by Juan Torres frantic shouting, and the dogs and the roosters. Lights in bedrooms all over town came on again as people attempted to discover the source of the disturbance.

There was no sleep for Manuel and Guadelupe the rest of that night. In the morning, Manuel left for work with the heartfelt plea by his wife to "Do something!" about the problem. When he entered the jail, he saw Juan, red eyed and distraught.

"Manuel, I have only three days left to go. PLEASE let me out now, I promise you I will no longer drink tequila. PLEASE!"

"This I cannot do Juan, I am already in trouble with the Federales."

It was clear to Manuel what he couldn't do, what he needed to know is what he COULD do. And of that, he hadn't a clue.

All that morning, townspeople dropped by the office asking what had happened the night before and Manuel told them. Jesus was very contrite, and apologized profusely to both Juan and Manuel. That day Manuel received a message from Ensenada. It contained both very good and very disturbing news. For his failure to adequately protect Federal property, a letter of reprimand was being put in his official record. Because most of the missing property had been recovered, no further punishment would be considered at this time. As for Jesus Arce, he is to pay a fine of $5,000 pesos, or spend 60 days in the jail at Bahia de los Angeles.

Manuel put down the message. He was greatly relieved that he was pretty well off the hook now, and would NEVER allow such a thing to happen again. But as for Jesus, caramba! He did not have 500 pesos of total net worth, let alone 5,000! Sixty days in jail was ok, but 59 more nights like the last one? Once again Manuel had a problem, a very large, very loud one. As he had feared, the day wore on, and once again the night came.

Manuel sat down with Jesus, and they had a heart to heart talk. Manuel reminded his prisoner that he could have been sent to prison in Ensenada, he was lucky only to be in jail here for two months. Jesus agreed, and promised to do anything he could to help solve the problem.

"I think you must learn to stay awake at night", Manuel said. "You can sleep in the daytime when the noise will be less annoying. Can you do that?"

Juan agreed, and from his cell urged "Yes Jesus! That is a good idea! What do you say?"

Jesus promised he would do his best. That night Manuel provided him with a sizeable stack of magazines, and left the light on in his cell. "Now remember Jesus, do not go to sleep until I return in the morning, understand?" He walked to his house and assured a very worried Guadalupe that all would be well. The good citizens of Bahia de los Angeles went to bed anticipating a good night's sleep, and all began well. About midnight however, the dreaded low pitched foghorn sounds began again. This was followed in short order by Juan's screams and demands for Jesus to wake up, which went unheeded. The roosters and dogs predictably took up the alarm and once again there was total chaos in the center of the pueblo. In desperation Guadalupe closed all the bedroom windows, but it was no use. The glass panes rattled with every snore, and in ten minutes the bedroom was sweltering. She had to open the windows, and the snores, followed by snorts and silences at unpredictable intervals, continued unabated.

Guadalupe and Manuel lay side by side in their bed on their backs staring at the ceiling, each trying to predict when the next snort would interrupt the uniform series of snores, knowing there would be no sleep for them that night. Soon there was an angry knocking on their door. It was their neighbors Maria and Ignacio Lopez, who were soon joined by Hortensia and Pablo Espinoza, and Pilar and Everrado Marques. They were all mad, very mad, and demanded that Manuel find some way to end this problem, or they would form their own lynch mob, storm the jail, and smother that foghorn with a pillow!

Manuel could see other neighbors approaching through the darkness, so he quickly agreed that he would fix the problem one way or another. He dressed and hurried to the jail. Juan was waiting for him, shaking, and it was obvious he was coming perilously close to a breakdown.

"Manuel, you have always wanted that double barreled shotgun I have. Amigo, please let me out of jail just a little early, and I will give it to you! Really, I will!"

Manuel ignored him. Again he had to shake Juan vigorously before the snoring finally stopped. Once again there was blessed silence.

"Oh no", said Jesus, "I was snoring again? I am sorry Manuel, I just fell asleep."

Manuel brightened. He had an idea. "No matter my friend. Do you play dominos?" Manuel let Jesus out of the cell and sat at his desk with him. He produced a set of dominos, and said

"Ok, let's play!" He knew he could not let Jesus fall asleep again.

The two men played one game of dominos after another until the sun finally shone over the islands in the gulf.

At just after six in the morning, the first angry citizens arrived at the jail. Manuel did his best to appease them, but the crowd continued to grow, and would not be mollified. Their mood had turned perilously nasty.

"We can elect another Delegado you know!" shouted one. This brought a spontaneous roar of approval from the throng gathered in front of the jail.

"You must DO something", another called, echoed many times by other voices, "Yes, DO something!"

Once again, Manuel stood on the porch in front of the jail and assured them all that he would indeed "do something" about the problem. This was met with sullen acceptance and threats such as "Well you had damned well better, or WE will!" again met with a murmur of approval from the crowd. Slowly the group melted away as people went home to try to get some sleep.

Manuel went back into the jail to be met once again by anguished pleas from Juan Arce. By now it was easy to see he had become a desperate man. He was shaking the door of his cell, and tears were beginning to flow down his cheeks. He mumbled over and over again, "Please Manuel, please, please, please!" Manuel opened the cell door and said "Go home Juan." Juan took the jailer's hand in both of his and said "Oh thank you, thank you!" And bolted out the door, taking the steps two at a time, and headed for his home. Again Manuel bade Jesus to come out of his cell and sit with him at his desk. The sheer desperation of his situation had stimulated what small amount of creativity he possessed, and he had at last come up with a plan. It was a desperate one, and one that if not carried out correctly could cost him his job.

"Jesus", he began, choosing his words slowly and deliberately. "I know that you cannot control this horrible snoring of yours – that is not your fault."

Jesus just shook his head sadly.

"But for me, and for many people in this village, it is a very bad problem. I have been thinking." he continued. "The Federales do not come to Bahia very often, and when they do, I almost always know ahead of time. Now, if I were to let you go home today, would you promise to come back to jail right away if I tell you to?"

Jesus was surprised. "Let me go home Manuel? But what if some one tells the Federales when they come?"

"Don't worry about that," Manuel assured him, "there is not a person in town that would want you to go back to jail again. If we are visited by the Federales, I will send some one to get you, and you must promise to come immediately and get into a cell. Do you agree?"

"Of course I do, and thank you! I assure you Manuel, I will not let you down!"

"You had better not," Manuel said menacingly, "for if you do, I will put you in jail again for only one or two nights.......and then I will turn you over to the people you heard outside the jail this morning!"

Jesus was clearly jarred as he contemplated this eventuality, and made a resolution to do exactly as he had been told.

The next night, and all the nights following, the grateful citizens of Bahia de los Angeles went back to sleeping comfortably through the night. The Federales did return once to do another inventory of the boats, and take some of them back to Ensenada. Jesus, as promised, had returned quickly to the jail cell, and the Federales found nothing amiss. The sixty day period finally ended, and Manuel breathed a sigh of relief. Guadalupe had her yard back, he still had his job, Jesus was back home, and the townspeople once more had confidence in his ability to competently discharge the duties of his office. No one ever breathed a word of the jailbreak, and it went undetected by the Federal Government of Mexico. Also, as the years went by, Manuel noticed that no one ever tried to build a house anywhere near Jesus' shack. This was very wise, he thought.

El Desengano

$\mathcal{T}$ here is a lot of gold south of Bahia de los Angeles, but there is even more to the north. Two of the largest and best producing mines in the Baja are located only a short distance apart, the Luz de Mexico, and El Desengano. The mines are at the foot of two mountain ranges, the Sierra La Assemblea, and the Sierra La Primavera. Lying between the two ranges is the beautiful Valle de Santa Ana. It is part of the large recently designated "Parque Natural Del Desierto Central de Baja California." Fortunately for me, the whole area is conveniently close to my home, and I can reach most places around the area within one day's journey.

In early May, one beautiful Baja spring day, I was preparing for a trip into the Mesa Colorado area just North of Desengano. I packed my truck following the routine I always used. I took my dry washer, shovels, picks, my metal detector, plus my rock hammer and other small equipment for field refining of the ore. In addition to these tools, I packed food and drink, most importantly water, tequila, beans, rice, canned meat, tortillas, fresh vegetables, and all the pots, pans, and utensils I needed to eat with. Also important were my tarp for shade, my sleeping pad and blankets, and a folding chair with arms.

As was my habit, I started out with the first light of day, alone, and with a multitude of thoughts and feelings assailing me all at once. First and foremost was anticipation. I never knew if this was the trip I would find that big mother lode, the rich vein, or maybe even some of that Jesuit gold. I knew chances were against me, but then, just maybe, if I was lucky.... A very strong competing feeling was one of caution and respect for the environment I was about to enter. The central Baja desert can be a harsh and unforgiving host to those who wish to visit its remote reaches. Mistakes, miscalculations, unforeseen events can be, and often are, fatal. For some, there has not been a second chance to get things right.

At times like these, when I was beginning a trip into the mountains, I always went with the understanding that I was entering natures realm, not man's. I was going in with the permission of the elements only, not the right that humans often assume. Mother Nature holds all the cards out there, make no mistake about it. You must take her into account at every step, and realize that situations that might be only irritating in populated areas, such as a truck in the sand, an animal bite, or a sudden illness. Such commonplace problems become much more dangerous when one is alone, cannot communicate, and not likely to be found for a long time. I have suffered injury, lost my truck, and come close to death by dehydration, and this has given me good reason to obey the laws of the desert faithfully. The Germans have a saying, "What ever does not kill me makes me stronger." This is certainly true in the desert. One or two real scares promote caution in the future like mere advice never could. As a seasoned desert rat, I was well aware of all this, and knew that my best chances of living to be an old miner was to be well prepared, knowledgeable, cautious, and most of all, damned lucky! Armed with these thoughts, I headed up into the mountains.

The first place on that trip I decided to make camp, I was very lucky in that I could drive all the way in, and had access to my truck. I could always make a more comfortable camp in these situations, without having to pack in a lot of heavy equipment and supplies. It took me until early afternoon to set up my camp, and I had only a couple of hours before dark to use for prospecting. I returned to camp at twilight, and began the preparations for supper that had become routine with me over the years. Part of setting up camp was to gather dead and dried wood for the campfire. I usually preferred mesquite for this, as it made better coals, but lots of other kinds worked fine if there was no mesquite nearby. After the fire was made, it was time to start preparing my dinner. I have made so many meals over so many years, that I have become a pretty good cook if I do say so myself. I know that around Bahia de los Angeles, I usually have plenty of company, sometimes uninvited, when I make one of my pots of locally famous seafood stew!

After dinner, I sit by the coals, and if I have not been bitten by a snake that day, I figure I have some of my snake-bite tequila available, so I might as well not let it go to waste. Sitting in my comfortable chair (with arms!), staring into the mesquite coals, I always do my best thinking – especially when the tequila begins to flow. I sit for a couple of hours under the clear Baja night sky, a billion stars shining down on my little campsite, and I think, and plan, and sometimes dream of that damned Jesuit gold. One of the main reasons I had chosen this area to explore, other than there was a good chance of finding placer gold, was that I felt that the missing Jesuit gold might have followed a trail north somewhere near this spot. As I sat night after night, staring into the coals, I tried to put together all the clues I had found so far, and to sequence in my mind what must have happened.

I could imagine the church at San Borja being temporarily unguarded between the time the Jesuits left for the coast, and the men of Galvez and Portola arrived to take over. The objects of gold on the altar were replaced with others of little worth. These gold objects were hurriedly packed onto burros and taken north to be kept beyond the reach of the new order. But the loss would have been soon discovered, and the missing objects searched for. Whoever took them would want to hide their cherished relics rather than see them taken north by the Franciscans. They could be retrieved when the situation had passed, and once more placed on a holy altar. Until the time was right, they must remain safe, and their location known only to a few of the faithful.

I knew all the Jesuit roads by heart, having prospected for years in the area between St. Gertrudis and San Borja. There were three in all, and in studying them, I had come to understand the tendencies of the mission dwellers, which path they probably would have taken. The Jesuits built no permanent roads north of San Borja, but they did have mission visitas to the north, and followed set paths between them. By taking time, thinking, and putting myself in their place, I was able to make a pretty good guess as to the route they would have followed north. I thought, looked at maps, and asked myself, if I had been them, which way would I have gone?

I turned in that night, anxious to put another piece in the puzzle the next day. In reality, the answer lay very close to where I was camped. At the time, I had no idea how close, but I was soon to find out.

I followed my usual morning routine the next day. I was up before the sun, stirred the coals and started another fire for breakfast. But first came the morning coffee, hot and steaming. I really looked forward to that first cup of coffee every morning, and the second and third as well. Somehow everything seems to taste better in the open air, and how I loved my breakfast! That morning I whipped up one of my favorites, huevos rancheros – with a good bit of hot sauce, beans, and tortillas. That kind of breakfast beats croissants and eggs Benedict on the Champs de Elyse in Paris, as far as I am concerned. After breakfast, I washed the pans and plates I had used with dry sand. It works well, try it some time. You don't need any water either. I gathered my backpack, rock hammer, cut myself a walking stick, and headed out for my day in the desert.

As I began my hike, it occurred to me that I was a truly lucky man. I was alone, but didn't mind that. I had no family, no job, no career, and no chance for advancement up society's ladder of success. That day, as with all others in the desert, all I had was my health, my knowledge of the desert, my love of the free life, and the equipment to find gold. I knew I would find gold, I always did. How much I did not know, nor can any miner. But I knew that often enough I would find a sufficient amount that I could choose to spend as much time as I wished at my beachfront home, sharing beers with my friends all day, spending every minute doing only what I chose to do. Or, I might elect to do what I did quite often, which was to pack up the truck and head for my childhood home in Las Vegas. I would trade the 100% real world, the world of sand and sun and mountains and animals, for the 100% artificial world of neon, carpets, glamour, glitter and hype of the Las Vegas strip. Actually, I loved them both. The difference was I could only take Las Vegas in small amounts at a time, and I wanted to be in the desert always. Las Vegas was like the dessert in my diet of life, but Baja was veggies and meat. Ok, I will admit some will see that as a copout. No wife, no kids, no obligations – a totally self indulgent and wasted life. Women especially think that. Maybe by their standards they are right, but I insist on living life by MY OWN standards, and anyone who meets me will attest to that. And if you are one of those, thanks for reading this book (hopefully having had to buy a copy), but with all due respect, go pound sand. I was not beginning a day of writing reports and kissing a bosses ass. I was heading into a day of looking for gold, and finding it! You are welcome to all the shoulds, woulds and coulds that society deals in.

I followed a path up the escarpment to a flat mesa. On the mesa there was a cardonal, a forest made up of cardon cactus. Cardon are one of the most striking of all the forms of plant life in Baja. They tend to grow together in groups, and can become huge in old age. They serve as a home for the ubiquitous cactus wren, a nice little bird that can be found wherever there are cardon cactuses. I sure like the wren better than those damned ravens. Those pinche black birds have caused me no end of trouble. If I leave any food at all uncovered at camp, they will peck their way through the thickest of packaging to get at it. They are damned smart opportunists. They look like crows, but have rounded tails, and can glide when they fly, which crows cannot do. They can be real pests!

I found a couple of places in the morning that showed good color, and took samples to refine later back at camp. At noon, I sat under the shade of a large cardon and ate the torta and orange I had brought for lunch. As was my habit, I stretched out after lunch for a short siesta. I have found by experience that for some reason beyond my understanding, the flies and gnats that can be very thick at times on the desert floor disappear for an hour or so at mid-day. Where they go, and why, I don't know. I do know their constant buzzing around my face makes sleeping impossible. So, I took advantage of this respite to take a nap. When I awoke, I continued my hike through the cardonal. I came upon a small clear area, and noticed on one side the dead remains of a huge cardon. It must have been hundreds of years old. At the base of the dead giant, the ground was very suspiciously hollowed, and of a slightly different color than the surrounding sands. My suspicions aroused, I marked the spot carefully in my mind, noted well all the visible landmarks, and planned to return the next day with my metal detector.

I did go back the next day, and as soon as I took a few sweeps over the area. I got a faint response from my detector. I had only removed about two feet of the overlying sand, when I discovered the first of a very large cache of bones. I recognized them as probably being burros, and spent the whole day excavating the pit. By the end of the day I had taken out the bones of two burros, some leather and buckles, and some almost completely decayed wood with rusty metal straps and nails. There was nothing of any value whatsoever in the pit, but I felt I had added another very important piece of evidence to substantiate my theory about the missing gold. I looked around the area, but could not find anything else of interest. The next day I returned to my prospecting, but my heart was no longer in it. I was intrigued to the point of being obsessed with tracking down that Jesuit gold. I was now convinced beyond a doubt that my theory was correct. I cut short my trip, returned home before I had intended to, and took out my maps of the area. I carefully noted the points at which I had found the candlestick and the dead burros. I then studied the terrain between the two points closely, and drew a line on the map that I felt represented the direction the treasure had taken. It was then possible to infer from that what the path north of my recent find might have been. I made the best guess I could, and then drew a circle around the spot that I wanted to search next. I began immediately to make preparations to reach that circle on the map, and continue my quest for the treasure of the Jesuits.

Antero Diaz and that Blasted Church

CHAPTER 18

One of the men I would often go prospecting with in my early days in Bahia de los Angeles was Antero Diaz. Antero had a lot of experience in gold mining, and had originally come to the bay for that purpose. As time went by, he shifted his focus from prospecting and mining to building and running the first rental rooms in town. At first these were just crude huts on the beach, but Antero proved to be a better businessman than miner, and the operation grew quickly. The bay being entirely vacant and unbuilt, he had no trouble securing title to most of the buildable land along the shoreline. He also laid claim to all the mineral rights in the area, but this was harder to enforce. He built a new building of cantera stone with several spacious rooms to rent. A restaurant, fleet of fishing pangas, dirt airstrip, grocery store, and gasoline station followed in quick order. Antero ran things outside the house, and his wife Cruz ran them inside. He took care of the boats and planes, and the running of the store. She saw to the rooms, the restaurant, and the family. They were both hard workers, and for some time the Diaz operation was the town, nothing else of any importance existed on the bay.

Bahia de los Angeles is, and always has been, a drop-dead beautiful place. In those days, the waters were teeming with fish of all kinds, with lots of turtles and sharks as well. The turtles were sold to markets in Ensenada and Tijuana, and the sharks were hunted for their fins and livers, most of which were sent to Japan. Yellowtail, Dorado, and tuna were sold to northern markets, and the sandy beaches were filled with clams a few inches below the surface at low tides. It was a natural paradise in the early days, with wonders of nature so abundant it attracted a lot of Americans. Most of the Americans flew in, landed on Diaz's strip and taxied right up to the hotel. That was long before the paved Highway 1 was completed, and arriving or leaving by road was only for the hardiest travelers. Transportation by air or water were the preferred modes.

As the Diaz complex drew more visitors each year, other Mexican families gravitated to the bay, most to work for Antero in one capacity or another. He needed women to clean the rooms, help with the cooking and do the washing. He needed men to operate the growing fleet of pangas, the type of boats used by the native fishermen, which he rented out to visiting gringos. Workman came to help build his rooms, and some settled down and stayed. So, as Bahia de los Angeles grew, most people who lived there owed friendship, allegiance and loyalty to Antero and the Diaz business complex. A few of the more adventurous Americans even had little beach houses built and began to visit the bay on a regular basis. At first, and for a long time, this was no problem. Antero treated everyone fairly, and did not use his position of power in a way that would alienate the people of the budding little town. His employees were regarded as family, and became very devoted to him Inevitably however, as the population grew, so did the number of people who had no debt to the Diaz family, and some of these began to grow a bit jealous of his power. Other businesses began to be established, and many of the newcomers were resentful of the influence that the Diaz family wielded. Being so remote, Bahia de los Angeles did not have much of a formal infrastructure. Antero himself informally filled many positions in the town, that of Mayor, police chief, fire marshal, and planning commission. A backlash against his power and influence was inevitable.

About that time, Antero had a great idea, as he was apt to do quite often. He was a free thinker, and not afraid to try new things that interested him. This time, he decided that the town needed a church. Of course, HE would build the church. He decided that it would not be any ordinary church, but one completely faced with onyx from the mines at El Marmol. Flushed with enthusiasm for his new project, he donated a piece of land for the church, and set about making arrangements for its construction. This unilateral decision proved to be the flashpoint for the anti-Diaz cabal in town. They had had enough, and went to work. They were bent on blocking the building of the church, and to for once assert control over Antero Diaz.

The closest place of any formal authority was Guerrero Negro, on the Pacific side of the peninsula, some 200 kilometers to the southwest of the bay. A contingent of indignant citizens went to the Catholic Diocese there, and registered their objections regarding the Diaz church. The Catholic church itself should have final say on the construction of a church, not a private citizen they asserted. Diaz would in effect be the private owner of a church. This would be a situation that organized religion did not intend to brook, the Padre at Guerrero Negro agreed. The determined little group from Bahia also visited the Delegado's office, and again, their pleas fell on sympathetic ears. The Delegado agreed that Bahia had grown beyond the stage at which it could, or should, be run by one man. It was time for bureaucracy to come to Bahia de los Angeles, and this man must at last be made to understand that he was controlled by higher authority.

A few weeks later, four official cars rumbled over the dirt road into the little town in a cloud of dust, and pulled up in front of the Diaz hotel. Among the visiting contingent were the Catholic priest, the Chief of Police, the Delegado, and the military commander, all from Guerrero Negro. They requested a visit with Antero, and he was glad to comply. As with many formal meetings in Mexico, the conversation dwelled for a while on the superficial and conven-tionalized trivialities of polite conversation. When the talk finally got around to the nitty-gritty, the message delivered was crystal clear. Antero was to cease and desist the building of the church at once. If he sought the permission of the church and the government, and adhered to their recommendations on the project, he could proceed. Diaz said very little in response, and the dignitary's motorcade left town that afternoon. Their job had been done. Authority had spoken.

Antero still had a lot of friends in the town, and a lot more that visited on a regular basis. He had put the word out that he needed onyx for the church, and pieces of the beautiful stone began to pour into town from a hundred sources. People arriving by car stopped at El marmol on the way, and bought some small slabs to donate to the church. Even pilots would bring some with them in their planes. Slowly the walls of the church went up, clad in shiny onyx. It most certainly would be one of the finest and most unique churches in all of Baja. Antero was very proud of it. Other eyes saw the church continuing to be constructed as well, and these were the eyes of a jealous, not proud people. Once again the proper authorities in Guerrero Negro were advised of the situation in Bahia. They were informed that their order to cease building the church was being ignored. Antero meanwhile, was convinced that the people from Guerrero Negro had had their say, and that the whole matter would be dropped and forgotten. He was wrong.

One day, quite unexpectedly, another motorcade from Guerrero Negro entered the town, this time it was made up of two jeeps, followed by three military trucks. The vehicles pulled up in front of the half-constructed church and parked. Soldiers jumped out with rifles at the ready, and stood guard around the building, while others went from house to house in the neighborhood near the church, and warned the people to evacuate the area immediately. Still other soldiers began carrying boxes from the trucks to the unfinished church, and stacking them inside. When the transfer had been completed, one last round of the nearby houses was made to be sure all the homes nearby had been vacated. With this final inspection completed, the trucks pulled away several hundred yards and halted. Minutes later two soldiers were seen running from the building. They leaped into a waiting jeep, and roared away to join the trucks.

For several moments there was dead silence. The soldiers waited. The townspeople waited also, wondering what in the world was going on. They didn't have to wonder long. An ear-splitting explosion shook the town, and a brilliant flash of orange from where the church had stood lit the sky. The ground shook as if from an earthquake, and shards of onyx like deadly missiles were hurled in all directions. Every window in town was shattered, and for a radius of hundreds of meters fragments of the ill-fated church made pock marks in any wall exposed to the blast. A giant cloud of dust and smoke enveloped the blast area, and for several seconds pieces of onyx and cement rained back to earth, pelting everything they landed on. For some time, no one dared to move. Never had such an explosion been experienced by any of them, and most were in a mild state of shock. After the rain of rocks and cement from the sky had ceased, the soldiers were the first to move. They examined the broken windows and dented sides of the trucks that had been exposed to the blast. Where the church had stood, there was now only a smoking crater four or five feet deep and thirty feet across.

The soldiers tried starting the vehicles, and found all were still running, so they boarded the trucks, and without further ado, the convoy left town. The military can probably not be blamed for what had happened, as they were just following orders. Also, it is understandable that they had not had much practice blowing things up, since explosives are expensive, and hard to come by in the Mexican Army. They had only used six or seven times the amount of explosives actually needed to destroy the church, but they had made the best guess they could. Besides, no one had been injured in the blast. One unlucky dog had been struck in the head by a shard of onyx however, and his soul was winging its way to the great kennel in the sky, but he was the only casualty.

The subtle suggestion from the soldiers was not lost on Antero, and he reluctantly but obediently discarded the idea of building the church. As a token of defiance however, he decided to scale down his idea, and erect a smaller building on his own property. Although the entire town was liberally sprinkled with onyx, it was not usable on the new building as there were few pieces larger than an inch or two left. Some people had not heard of the blast however, and more onyx continued to reach Bahia. It was enough to face the smaller building. No complaint was lodged concerning the construction of the chapel. The good citizens of Bahia de los Angeles all held their breath for some time, but as yet the military has not paid a similar visit. The onyx chapel of Bahia de los Angeles may be seen to this day, facing the courtyard next to the Diaz restaurant.

Green Valley

*T*here are some drop-dead beautiful places in the central Baja, but for my money, one of the most beautiful is the palm oasis at Green Valley. I have spent a lot of time there and thereabouts in my wanderings through the desert. One needs only a single trip into the desert to appreciate the sight of green palms and clear blue water after hours of trekking through the parched desert. And that goes double for some one who spends his whole life in the dry barancas of the Baja. Such is the feeling I always get when heading for Green Valley. I still remember my first trip, not for the beauty of the place, or the cool water, or the shade it has to offer, but for a far different reason. I almost died of thirst that first visit, because of a silly mistake, one that I never made again. I lost my truck!

It all began innocently enough. A friend of mine, another habitual desert rat, and sometimes partner, had told me of the place, and we finally chose a time and made all the preparations to go and explore it. It was near an area that we knew had produced a good amount of placer gold, and we hoped we could find some more good spots to prospect. My friend had estimated that we could drive close enough to the oasis to park the truck and walk in and back out again in one day. As we were to find out, he was wrong!

We started out before dawn one summer morning, and drove over increasingly less used roads, which finally degenerated into just ruts in the ground, until we found our way blocked by an impassable area of shifting dunes. We could drive no further, so as was my custom, I looked for a place to hide my truck while we were away. If we left it out in the open, it, and all its contents, would be fair game for anyone who happened upon it. We were, granted, in a very remote and seldom visited spot, but I still preferred to take no chances. We finally found a little ravine, pulled the truck in, and covered it with mesquite branches. We did a good job of hiding it – as we were to later discover to our chagrin, too good!

As we planned to be back at the truck by nightfall, and we had a long hike ahead of us, we took minimal equipment. We also new there would be potable water available when we arrived at the oasis, so we took only one gallon of drinking water in a plastic bottle. Even only a gallon of water is heavy – it weighs eight pounds. When you are hiking through the desert on a summer day, every pound adds to your toil. So, with our gallon of water, our prospecting tools, and high spirits, we started out on my first and most memorable trip to Green Valley.

The sun rose higher in the eastern sky as we started across the dunes, and soon we were sweating profusely on a triple digit temperature day. We were both seasoned desert wanderers, and took the heat in stride. It was slow going through the loose sands of the dunes, but we could see in the distance an elevated plateau that promised better footing, and faster progress. My partner advised me that the oasis was just on the far side of the mesa. Quick calculation of time and distance convinced me that we could easily reach the palm canyon ahead, and return before nightfall.

We reached the foot of the plateau, which stretched for miles to both our right and left, and scrambled up the slope. To our satisfaction, we saw that it was not far to the other side of the plateau. It was only a couple of miles, and the going was much easier, enabling us to reach the far side in less than a half an hour of hiking. We approached expecting to look down upon the beautiful, inviting scene the oasis would provide after our long hot walk. What we saw when we looked down from the cliff, was not palm trees and water, but another, lower elevated tabletop mesa stretching out before us. We were very disappointed, and had to make a decision as to whether or not we should proceed. After discussing the situation, we decided to go ahead and cross this mesa, and if the oasis was not on the other side, we would return to the truck and try again. It was still relatively early in the day, we had plenty of water left, and we had already come this far, so we decided to press on.

After making the choice to continue, our first task was to find a place along the cliff that was a little less steep, so that we could descend to the lower mesa. We found a spot nearby, but had to more or less slide down on the seat of our pants as there was a lot of loose rock and gravel, and the cliff was very steep. After reaching the bottom, we traversed the mesa with no problems, and arriving at the far side, looked down upon what we had expected to see earlier. There are some scenes so awesome and wonderful to behold that the thrill of experiencing them never seems to diminish. One such scene that never ceases to give me goose bumps is the first glimpse one gets of Bahia de los Angeles. After many miles of dry desert, one tops a gentle rise and is treated in an instant to the sight of beautiful blue waters and an island dotted bay. It is a sweeping panorama of the best that nature has to offer. It is the same way for me with the palm canyon oases of Yubay, and now Green Valley as well.

We reached the pool of clear cool water among the forty foot palms, and relaxed a while in the shade after our long hike in. We ate a lunch that we had brought with us. It had taken us much longer to reach the place than we had originally calculated, and we knew that we had only a short time to look around for signs of gold. We went our separate ways, and agreed that we would meet back at camp in two hours. When we did meet up at the appointed time, we were both very encouraged by what we had found. Several of our samples had shown good color, and we were anxious to continue collecting. We faced yet another decision. We had not planned nor provided for an overnight stay. The pros and cons of our situation were clear. On the minus side, we had no food, save on orange that I had not eaten at lunch. We also lacked blankets or sleeping bags, and would have to spend the night on the ground. The plus side was much more persuasive. We had plenty of fresh water, it was the middle of the summer so the night would be hot, blankets would not be used even if we had them, and neither of us were strangers to sleeping on the sand. All of these perks were insignificant to the biggest one we both knew would prevail – if we stayed overnight, we got to do some more prospecting! The case was closed immediately, and we both went out to prospect again until dark. We could always replenish our water in the morning, and still have time to do a little more looking around before we left. We now knew the way back, and how long it would take. All we had to do was follow our footsteps back out. An unwarranted confidence prevailed. We retired for the night, and were lulled to sleep by the sounds of the desert birds that made the waterhole their home. A nice cooling wind came up during the night, as it often does in this area, and made the heat more bearable, almost pleasant. We awoke the next morning. Neither of us was the worse for wear after out night under the palms. Probably the thing I missed the most was my habitual cup of hot coffee. We had plenty of water, and could easily have made a fire, but we had no pot, cups, or coffee with us. We were in out common element however, there were signs of gold all around us, and we were anxious to get started again. After three hours of productive prospecting we reluctantly left our little paradise, and headed back across the first mesa on our way home. The place had been so promising, that we both had several samples of black sand that showed good color. It was certain we would return quickly if what we had panned out was as good as we expected. The samples were very heavy, along with our replenished gallon of fresh water, but we made good time and were on schedule to reach the truck before dark. We had all we needed in the truck, and would spend a comfortable night there before driving out the next morning. We looked forward to an evening of good food, and a Tequila or two, followed by a comfortable night's rest dreaming of the great sand ores we had found.

The day was even hotter than the day before, and our load heavy as we trudged on toward the cliff we had descended. Neither of us looked forward to having to go up the steep slope to the plateau. The level of the water in the jug went constantly lower as we replaced by necessity moisture in our system that sweat and our breath had removed. We had to look quite a while for a place that we could manage to climb to the top, but finally found one. Again, time was a factor as the sun had long passed its zenith and we had only a couple of hours of daylight. Worse, the water was almost gone. The hardest part of the walk was behind us though, and there was only the narrow plateau and the dunes between us and the truck. In the truck, waiting for us, was the thirty gallons of fresh water I always took with me on my trips. Knowing this convinced us it was safe, once we had reached the dunes, to drink the last of the water. It would take us less than an hour to cross the dunes and arrive back at the hidden truck.

Crossing the dunes, we made straight for the ravine in which we thought we had left the truck. We found the ravine, but the truck was not there. We were both certain this was the spot. Had some one happened upon it, and made off with it? That did not seem possible, as we did not see any tire tracks, nor did we find the pile of mesquite branches we had used to hide it. It was necessary at that point to face the truth. When we had strayed from our original path to find a way up the escarpment to the plateau, we had failed to return to our correct position, and had crossed the dunes far from our point of entry. It was time to face facts. We were in a dangerous, potentially life threatening, situation. We were out of water, hungry, tired, and quickly becoming dehydrated. There was only enough time to look at two other close by ravines before nightfall. Both proved fruitless. With the coming of dark, we had no choice but to spend yet another night sleeping on the sand, but this time without an endless supply of water close at hand.

When we awoke the next morning, the seriousness of our situation was obvious. The sun was already scorching after only a few minutes after rising above the hills to the East. We were hungry, tired, concerned, and very angry at ourselves for being in this situation by our own doing. The first priority was of course to get water. There was only one source of water available to us, and that was in the bed of my pickup truck. We had to find that truck, and find it fast, or we were in big trouble. After searching through several ravines in the area with no success, we decided to split up. If both of us were looking independently, we could cover twice as much ground. Whoever found the truck would return to our camp of the night before with water. We left our heavy sample ores, and set out to continue the search.

I chose to head in a direction that I was almost sure was the right way, and he headed in the other. The truck had to be within a distance of two or three miles in either direction. We regretted greatly the care with which we had hidden it. I searched ravine after ravine that morning, each was empty, and seemed to be mocking me. By noon my mouth had gone completely dry, I was having a hard time swallowing, and knew that I was depleting the salt in my body to a dangerous level by two days of loss in sweat. At last my thirst was stronger than my desire to continue looking for the truck. I found a good sized barrel cactus, and having no knife, smashed it open with my rock hammer. Ripping off a chunk of the pulp in the center of the cactus, I could feel the cool liquid it contained dripping down my fingers. I eagerly sucked on the pulpy mass, and immediately received both a reward and a punishment. The reward was that the liquid at once lubricated my mouth and throat, and provided a welcome relief to my parched tissues. The punishment was that it was some of the bitterest stuff I have ever tasted! Yeeechh! Actually drinking the stuff seemed out of the question. There were only a few drops to be squeezed from each handful, and they were so vile that I doubted I could keep much down. Maybe later I would have to try, but for right now, relief from the dryness and pain of my mouth and throat would have to do.

No sooner that I had finished sucking liquid out of my chunks of cactus, and was preparing to continue my search, than I heard one of the sweetest sounds I have ever heard in my life! I heard the not too distant sound of my truck's horn. He had found it! My spirits were lifted in an instant, and I headed pell-mell toward that wonderful sound. He kept blowing the horn every couple of minutes, making it easier for me to home in on his location. I found him sitting on a rock near the truck, holding a gallon container of water that was three quarters gone. He offered me the jug, but I walked right past him, grabbed another container out of the bed of the truck, ripped the top off, and poured water into over, and around my mouth. Champagne has never tasted better to any human being than that water did to me. As soon as I had emptied the container, half of it in me, half on me, I got some salt tablets out of the truck and we both took several. There was still plenty of time to get back to Bahia de los Angeles if we left right away, but that would mean leaving our ore samples behind. We sat looking at each other silently for a moment, then without a word, we both began preparations for going back to our previous night's campsite for the samples. We were, after all, miners. The desert had managed to scare the hell out of us, but it had not beaten us, and we would not let it cheat us of our original goal. We got out samples, made a comfortable camp by the truck, almost finished a whole bottle of tequila between us that evening, and in the morning returned to town. When asked what took us so long, we just casually mentioned that we had just decided to stay a couple of extra nights – no problem. We had our reputations to think of you know!

A Reporter From the San Diego Union Tribune

CHAPTER 20

$\mathcal{I}$ answered the knock on my door to find a fresh-faced kid of about 20 years of age smiling at me.

"You Mr. Hill?" he asked.

"Yeah, come on in."

"Thanks! I want to visit one of the gold mines around here, and write a story about it. My name is Scott. How do you do!"

He shook my hand confidently, and continued "I am a reporter for the Union-Tribune newspaper in San Diego. Everybody I talk to around here says you are the guy who knows all about the mines in this area."

" Well, after working these mountains for three decades I should know a little something about them" I said. "Is this a paying job?" I knew full well it wasn't.

"No, but I will send you a copy of the story when it is published in the paper." he said hopefully.

I kind of liked the kid instinctively. He was a little brash and wet behind the ears, but seemed intelligent enough. I was ready for a little walk up the mountain anyway, so I agreed to meet him the next morning. Actually, I found out from some of his friends later that evening that he wasn't really a reporter for the San Diego U.T., yet anyway, but a journalism major at San Diego State University. He wanted to have a story to submit to the Union Tribune for publication. Even though he had not been completely honest with me, I decided I would go anyway. The next morning he arrived at my house at the exact hour agreed upon, and we got into my pickup and headed for the mountains and the nearby gold mines.

I had decided to take him up to Las Flores, which was an ore processing site for several of the many mines in the area, the largest of which was the famous San Juan mine. There had been a lot of gold taken out of the San Juan in its day before it was played out. All of the canyons in the vicinity of Las Flores had mines, and I had decided to show him one that was fairly accessible, called El Tigre. We parked the truck, and started climbing the steep canyon slopes that led up to the mines. We passed the first of two small graveyards in the area. Scott took down all the names and dates that were still legible on the ancient markers using a pad and pen that he carried in his shirt pocket. I explained to him how hard the life of the miners was, and all the dangers that had claimed those who were buried there. He listened intently, and took copious notes on everything I said. I thought he looked very reporter-like, and that maybe one day he actually would be one, but I never let on that I knew he had misled me.

After another two hours of walking the steep trails further into the canyons, and higher above the valley floor, we came to a fork in the trail. Paths led further up to the left and to the right, and between them, high on a knoll was a flat area where the miners had established a base camp many years ago. We took the fork to the right, and headed toward El Tigre. When we got half way up, there was a trail that took off toward the knoll. Scott said he wanted to go up and see the remains of the camp, and take some photographs from up there. I said I would go ahead on to El Tigre, which was just a couple of miles further up the trail, and he could catch up with me there. He agreed, and headed up toward the knoll.

I reached El Tigre after another solid hour of walking. It was the same as I had remembered from so many years ago when it had been in its hay day. The vein it contained had initially been very rich with gold deposits, and had attracted a lot of attention at first. Unfortunately, it had proven to be small in size, and the amount of good ore produced had diminished rapidly, until the mine was finally abandoned. I walked in to the open shaft a few feet until the sunlight from the entrance grew dim. I heard some rustling and scratching coming from the interior of the mine. As my eyes became accustomed to the dim light, I could see what was causing the noise. Desert rats were using the cave as a refuge from the burning sun of the Baja summer. They had dragged in piles of Cholla cactus, one of their favorite foods. The floor of the mine ahead was packed with the stuff. Cholla is one of the most feared cacti in the Baja. The spines are sharp, and curved on the end like a fish hook, so if they pierce the flesh of an animal or person, they are extremely difficult to remove without causing more damage to the skin. I knew immediately that Scott the 'reporter' and I would have to visit another mine, not this one.

I decided to wait there for him to arrive so I could explain the situation. Sitting in the shade, drinking some of my water, I waited. For almost two hours I enjoyed the view and the beautiful day. When Scott still had not arrived, I was concerned that something had happened, and decided to go find out what was keeping him. I gathered my things and headed back down the trail. Reaching the spur trail that led to the knoll, still there was no sign of my companion. As I started up the trail to the knoll above, I noted how it had deteriorated in the decades it had lain in disuse. I came to a spot on the trail where the ground showed a recent disturbance, and at the same moment heard a faint cry – "Help". Not really a yell, more of a hoarse whisper. Looking down over the edge of the trail, I saw Scott. He was lying flat on his back, arms and legs spread, body rigid and unmoving.

"Help" again, hardly audible. I sized up the situation quickly He was about half way between the trail from which he had fallen, and the lip of the cliff that descended straight into the canyon below. I didn't blame him a bit for being literally scared stiff. At the same time, I knew that his situation, although dangerous, was quite a common occurrence for anyone who spent time in these mountains. It had happened to me a dozen times or more, and I knew what to do.

I climbed down to Scott, and lay beside him. He was paralyzed by fear, and his eyes were glazed, not looking at me at all. I knew the first thing I had to do was get his attention, to be able to communicate with him. After that, the job was to get him turned around onto his stomach for the crawl back up to the trail.

He seemed a little encouraged by the fact that I had found him, but still refused to move or even make eye contact with me. I talked to him for a few minutes, reassuring him. He suddenly blurted out "My whole life flashed before my eyes!" Eager to keep him talking, and get his mind off the edge of the cliff below us, I told him that the same thing had happened to me. He finally looked at me. "It did? Really?"

"Yes", I assured him "It really did!"

" I saw stuff from when I was a kid! When I first got my dog, graduation from high school, like that." We were making progress.

"Mine was a little different" I said. He looked at me. "You know how when you are in a bar, or at a party, and are hitting on a good looking girl?" He nodded. "And then you ask for her telephone number and she gives it to you, and then you get so drunk you can't remember it the next morning?" He looked a bit confused. "Well, right then, at that moment, all those old numbers that I had forgotten flashed before my eyes. It was the damnedest thing! He laughed, and I knew we would be ok from there on out. Slowly I got him turned around and headed back up the embankment to the trail. We went very very slowly, with me telling him when to move a hand or a foot, and exactly where to place it. Even after we had arrived back in town, Scott was still pale, shaking, and unsteady. He had been through a real ordeal, and had had quite enough of the desert.

We never did get to see a goldmine that day, and I doubt if that young man ever will attempt to see one the rest of his life. He left Bahia the next day. I never did get his last name. For a long time, whenever I saw a story by a reporter named Scott, I would wonder if it was him. None of the stories have ever been about visiting gold mines!

The jail building at Las Flores still stands today. If you look closely, in the background to the left can be seen some of the remains of the reworked San Juan tailings.

The old grave at Las Flores. Every spring it is covered with beautiful desert flowers.

My favorite place in Bahia de los Angeles, the Villa Bahia hotel. This little jewel of a place can be reached at: ***www.villabahia.com.*** *Tell them Herman sent you!*

This is the only known photo of the original onyx church under construction.

Shown here is the chapel faced with onyx from El Marmol. It still stands today next to the Diaz store – a monument to Antero's determination!

This is one of the original steam engines from the San Juan mine. These were used to haul ore. The boys shown here now have grandchildren this age!

This is a typical trail leading between remote ranchos in central Baja. It is passable by foot,   burro, or horse, but not by car or truck.

We are still full of high hopes, me included, as we set out to find my lost vein.

Working the faces of sheer cliffs is a gold miners occupational hazard. It is from a cliff much like this one that I took my worst fall.

My Lost Vein

$\mathcal{I}$ suppose everybody has had times in their lives in which they were presented with some golden opportunity they did not take advantage of, and have regretted the rest of their lives not having done so. It might be a relationship that was terminated too soon, a stock that was not bought before the price went sky high, or a car sold cheap that became a classic. I had a missed opportunity that has haunted my memory for some years, and it was truly a 'golden' opportunity. In short, I lost a pretty big pile of gold!

It was the middle of the Baja winter, and at 5,000 feet of elevation, where I was prospecting, it can get mighty chilly. To add to the misery, there was a misty rain that made everything in my camp soggy and even colder. I had been out almost two weeks already on this trip and was ready both psychologically and physically to go back down the mountain to the warmth and comfort of my home in Bahia de los Angeles. I resolved as I arose from my damp blankets and fixed coffee with frigid fingers, that I would pack up at the end of the day and leave the next morning with the first light of dawn.

That gave me one more day to finish exploring the area I had been working. My prospecting had been very promising indeed, and I had managed to squeeze out several grams of gold each day, including some good-sized nuggets. I was determined to have one more good day of tricking the mountains out of their hidden sprinklings of gold, and so I headed for the last area I had still to cover. I hiked up a steep canyon and came to a beautiful little meadow covered with blue and yellow and white desert flowers. The bees were busy collecting pollen and then buzzing off around the side of the mountain. Probably a lot of good honey somewhere around, if I was going to stay longer I might have gone looking for it. Too bad I couldn't get my truck a little closer up here, I thought. It would make a perfect spot to set up camp.

On one side of the meadow, the seasonal rains had washed out a good-sized baranca, a flood channel cut into the soil by fast moving water. I saw that a vein of quartz has been exposed along one side of the baranca, a large one. As I got closer, I saw a sight that always has, and always will, set the heart of a miner pounding. I saw the color of gold! The mist made the rocks shiny, and from thirty feet away I could see several glints of the deep yellow of high quality gold. I had hit it! I was in a gold miner's dream. I could collect more gold in twenty minutes from this one spot than I had in the previous two weeks of working ten hours a day.

If there was this much gold exposed on the outside of the vein, I knew that there was probably an equal or greater amount to be had if I could follow the quartz further into the mountain. I also knew that this outcropping had been weathering and wearing down for thousands of years, and there would be a lot of gold in both nuggets and small grains to be had if I could follow the path of gravity down the baranca. Being heavier, the gold would have migrated down into the bedrock below over centuries of wind and rain. I knew from both experience and instinct that if I could bring in picks and shovels, I could remove the overburden. Once I got to the bedrock, the gold would be found in the cracks and crevices where gravity had caused it to lodge.

All of this was of course not possible at the time. I was just prospecting, not mining, and I did not have any of my equipment for extracting gold with me. I had only my rock hammer, which I used the rest of the morning to break off pieces of the gold-bearing quartz. By early afternoon I had collected as many samples as I could carry in my backpack, and believe me, it was good ore. It would be a while before I would be able to return, so I took time to kick dirt from above into the baranca until the quartz vein was covered. I was tempted to pack up immediately and head for home, but I knew I couldn't make it out of the mountains before dark, and it is extremely dangerous to drive at night in the mountains, especially when the ground is wet and muddy. So, with the first light of day, I was up and making a fresh pot of coffee. I packed the truck carefully for the trip down the mountain and hid the backpack full of gold ore under some tools and the spare tire in the bed of the truck.

I had developed the habit over the years of hiding my tire tracks when leaving a place that I didn't want to be found by anyone else. I cut off several short lengths of mesquite branches and tied them securely to the back bumper so they would drag along on the ground behind me. This effectively obscured my tire tracks, even in the mud, preventing anyone from easily following my path. It forced me to drive very slowly, and it was a long trip out of the mountains and onto a well-traveled dirt road leading to Green Valley and then on to Bahia de los Angeles. When I reached this road, I removed the mesquite branches. The thought of a cold beer and a warm shower drew me like a magnet to my beloved beachfront home. As always, the comforts of being at home were very welcome after time spent out in the desert. I had an icy Corona, talked with some of my neighbors who happened by, and made a stew for supper. It was good to be home.

After spending a warm and comfortable night in my own bed, I was awakened the next morning by a knock on my door. It was a neighbor with an important message from my home in Las Vegas. There had been a serious illness in my family and I was needed right away. I again loaded up my truck and immediately set out on the two-day trip home. As it turned out, I had to stay much longer than I had hoped. My uncle had passed away and there was much family business to be attended to. Months later, when I returned home to central Baja, I myself became ill and for another several months did not feel up to the rigors of hiking the mountains with a heavy pack.

During this time, I did further processing on a small part of the ore sample I had collected almost a year before and sent it north with a friend to be assayed. I got the results a couple of weeks later, and they were even better than I expected. It was a very high quality gold, almost pure. I was recovering from my illness, but still not up to the level of energy it would take for weeks of work at high elevations. I was anxious to get back to the spot again though and an opportunity to do so soon presented itself.

In Bahia de los Angeles, there is a turtle rescue program helping to preserve the stock of green leatherneck and hawksbill species of the gentle giants. They once swam the waters of the gulf in impressive numbers, but are easy to catch and were soon hunted almost to extinction. The site is very popular among ecology-minded students from the United States and is visited frequently by groups from schools and clubs. I used to help out with the care of the turtles on a volunteer basis, as did many of the Americans who lived in the little village of Bahia. One morning I was attending to my turtle-feeding duties, observed closely by a small covey of lovely young ladies from California. One asked me what I did for a living, and I told her. Immediately the interest and conversation turned from turtles to gold. I invited them to visit my home later that day and promised to show them some real gold from the mountains that surround the bay.

They showed up at my door as promised, and I was soon passing cold Cokes and gold nuggets around to all. They were fascinated by the gold and my ability to find it. They looked at me with admiration and respect, and flattered me by showing rapt attention to everything I said. "You mean you just find it on the ground and pick it up?" one wide-eyed blonde beauty asked. I explained that it was not quite *that* easy. And then I got an idea. "Would you like to go see where I found this gold?" I got an enthusiastic positive response from each of these unfurling rosebuds seated on my patio, and we immediately began making plans. They all had the hiking boots, sleeping bags, and excess energy that would be required for the trip. I looked forward to being the intrepid leader who would guide the party to the sparkling treasure I knew awaited us. I anticipated the awe and admiration that would be heaped upon me when I humbly and nonchalantly used my superior skills to locate the gold. This was going to be fun. I knew where the gold was and that there was lots of it, but they would think I could just go find a lode whenever the spirit moved me.

On the appointed morning, we all piled into two four-wheel drive pickups and were on our way. I knew that there were so many turns and branching canyons ahead of us that none of them would be able to remember the way. Even to an experienced miner, but especially to novices such as these girls, desert canyons and gulches can look a lot alike. There is often not much to mark one as different from another.

Before GPS satellites, knowing and maintaining your exact location was extremely difficult in the vastness of the trackless desert. No, I had no fear of them being able to remember and pass on to others the location of my cache of gold.

All that day, we climbed higher and higher into the mountains. There were no tire tracks since I had ably erased them on my way out. Even after almost a year, I would normally have been able to locate small preserved patches of my unique tread marks in hardened mud. But, I was denied even these slight clues and could only guess as to where I had parked my truck on the original trip. By evening, I was sure we had come far enough, but I still could not recognize my old campsite. I finally had to choose a spot that looked about right and so we parked the trucks. We built a campfire, the girls cooked a great evening meal, and we passed around a bottle of tequila before we all turned in for the night. I felt slightly uneasy, as my plan was not exactly on track, but I still was confident that the next day I would recognize some clue and would find the meadow again. We all arose early, had a great breakfast, and headed up higher into the mountains on foot. The mood among the youngsters was bright with anticipation. Today was the day they were going to learn how to find gold. We had only the one day, as we had to head back down to town the next day because the girls were scheduled to return home to Los Angeles (the BIG Los Angeles).

As the day wore on, I led them up one canyon after another without locating the meadow. My plan to win their respect and admiration was beginning to be replaced by sinking hope and increasing desperation. Oh how I would have loved to suddenly stumble onto that beautiful meadow, show them the gold, and humbly accept the smiles of respect and, yes, even hero worship, on their shining young faces. But, I couldn't find it. I could almost hear the mountain gods roaring their derisive laughter at me for having even dared to make finding their hidden secrets look easy. It was as if I was being taught a lesson by nature – which only those chosen are allowed to find the mountains riches. It is a privilege not to be trifled with. I had attempted to use a ruse to lead these girls to believe finding gold was easy, and nature was teaching me a lesson. It was *not* easy to find gold, and the mountain gods were giving me my comeuppance in front of this impressionable group.

I would be exposed as a braggart and a liar, a pathetic old man who had tried and failed.

I had but one chance to snatch victory from this impending defeat. I had to find some other spot that had gold. There was barely enough time to make it back to the trucks and our camp before nightfall, so I started back down the mountain, using an alternate route. It seemed that luck was with me, as I spotted another vein of quartz exposed on the side of a small eroded ridge above a sandy draw. Aha! There was still a chance! I might not be exposed as an abject scoundrel after all, but have an exalted place in the memory of these girls for the rest of their lives. I began chipping away at the quartz with my rock hammer, but saw nothing. I selected several spots along the quartz seam, and tried them all – with no results. I could sense the interest in the group around me fading, as I took sample after sample, but finding nothing. At last, I cracked off one piece of quartz, and detected a tiny glint of yellow deep in a crevice of the sample. "Here," I bellowed, "Here is your gold!" They all passed the sample around, but were singularly unimpressed. "Is that little thing in there gold?" one asked. "It isn't as big as the ones you showed us at your house." noted? complained? another. With diminishing hopes I took several more samples, none of which had gold. At last, we had no more time. We had to start back for the trucks.

Suffice it to say that the general esteem in which I had been previously held was largely absent that night and the following day on the way home. I didn't bother with hiding our tracks on the way out. The girls all politely thanked me when we reached Bahia. The next morning they were gone, and I haven't seen or heard from any of them since. I can only imagine that they consider gold very hard to find, and have no confidence in my ability to find it.

I really hate to admit it, but I never did find that damned meadow again. I went up there several times but quit looking after being frustrated by throwing away good time after bad, trying to find that quartz seam that I hid too well. As far as I know, it's still there. I am not a hard rock miner, so I wouldn't have followed the vein too far into the mountain, but I do know that there were at least a couple kilos of gold that I could have reached easily with what equipment I could pack in by myself. Not only that, but if I could have worked that sandy draw, removed the overburden and gotten down to the bedrock, I'll bet I could have come up with a lot more in small grains too.

If you would like to try to find that blasted meadow, buy 100 copies of my book and I will show you the general area where it is. I can't show you *exactly* where it is, because if I could, I'd go dig it up myself!

The Gold Miner's Delimma

CHAPTER 22

$\mathcal{T}$ here is one thing I can tell you for sure after a lifetime of mining for gold. People treat you very differently when you actually have the gold in your hand, than they do when you are just talking about it. Believe me, I know, because I have experienced it uncountable times.

People almost always are very skeptical when a miner talks of gold he wants to look for, and even gold he has found in the past.

Their attitude is "Prove what you say."

My reaction to them is "Screw you. Why do you think I should have to prove anything to you?"

You can tell people your son is a Senator, you wrote five books on nuclear physics, or you won the lottery last year, and they will accept it as fact. Tell them you took a kilo of gold out of a particular spot, and they will become condescending and patronizing. "Sure you did Herman, sure.", with a guarded wink to others.

Well, to Hell with them all. I know the truth, and I don't really care whether they believe it or not.

It is different when one miner talks to another. No miner would think of asking another he has just met exactly how much gold he found, and exactly where. He found the gold, good for him, you are glad for him. Where, and how much, is HIS business, not yours.

And there is a good reason for this. Once you have actually found the gold, and can show it, EVERYBODY not only believes it, but immediately tries to figure out a way to get some of it from you. They are not anxious to bankroll you when you leave to go mining, but if you return with gold, they are all chomping at the bit to deal. They all want to become your partner, or somehow get a piece of it for themselves. Most miners I know don't think like that, and it is for this reason that I have learned that the only people to speak openly and candidly about some things are other miners. Even then, there are things left unsaid, and for good reason.

What would my life be like if I was completely candid about my prospecting? Just suppose for a moment, that when I came down from the mountains with, let's say, twenty five grams of gold that I had worked for days to find and process, I showed it to anyone I saw. Not that I, or any other miner in his right mind, would be stupid enough to do this. First off, if I showed the wrong person, especially in a remote place, I might well wind up hit over the head and left to die after being relieved of the gold. If I showed even my friends in Bahia de los Angeles, I would be politely reminded, that now that I was rich, I should remember my friends, and help them out. The motor on Ramon's boat is broken, and he needs money to buy parts to repair it. Victoria's mother needs to go to San Quintin for an operation, and they will need money for gas to get her up there. And on, and on, and so forth ad infinitum. Nugget by nugget, good deed by good deed, my poke is reduced to zero.

For arguments sake, let's say that I avoid these pitfalls by actually keeping my mouth shut until I get home. But, I am still open and honest, and mention to the president of the Ejido how much gold I have found.

"Ah, my friend Herman, that gold came from ejido land, no?" According to our rules (that he just made up) half of that gold goes to the ejido. (In actuality, half of whatever I gave him would go to the ejido, the other half to fund his daughter's quincinera.)

But, with luck, I avoid the presidente, and instead run into the Delegado of the town. and he sees the gold.

"Senor Hill, you know well that the State of Baja California Norte demands 40% of whatever you find. This land belongs to them, what makes you think the gold is all yours just because you found it? I will give it to them so you can avoid all the paperwork and the trip to Ensenada that would be necessary. Luckily, I am going up there next week myself."

We take out his 40%, which looks more like about half to me, and he leaves the next week for Ensenada. I know that I will never see the paperwork that he has warned me about. When he arrives in Ensenada, he decides to get new tires and a paint job for his pickup truck rather than give the state its 25% share.

But no, I avoid him too. On my way up to Ensenada, a Federale sees the mining equipment in the back of my truck, and stops me to ask some questions. Of COURSE, being an honest person, I show him the gold.

He looks at it, and replies "Senor Hill, I am sorry, but I will have to place you under arrest. You will come with me to the carcel, and we will have to impound your truck and all your equipment."

Why?", I ask. "We have reports of stolen gold in Guerrero Negro. But if this gold is yours, you have nothing to worry about. Can you please show me your permit from the Federal Government of Mexico to mine gold on their land?"

Well, of course, I don't think there even is such a permit, but in any event, I don't have one, and am now in a lot of trouble. My car will be impounded, I will go to jail and face stiff fines, and I will be lucky if I am not thrown in the La Mesa Prison in Tijuana for stealing the gold.

Fortunately for me, the Federale sees a way out of my predicament.

"This is too bad for you Senor Hill. I don't want to see all these bad things happen to you. Perhaps if you were to give the gold back, so it could be returned to its owner......" "But I didn't steal it!" I protest self-rightously.

"Ok" he says, "Then follow me to San Quintin. You can stay there in the carcel until we can transport you to Ensenada for your trial, which should only take a few months, and then if you are innocent you can return home and come and pick up your truck and belongings. No problem!"

I begin to see things his way, and hand over the gold. That way I return to my home, rather than the jail. The Federale uses the gold to buy some more calves for his father-in-laws ranch, where he hopes to retire one day.

But, to continue the scenario, I avoid this pitfall as well, keep the gold in my pocket, and actually make it all the way to the border. There, entering the land of the free, I see armed men with drug sniffing dogs patrolling up and down the lines of cars. They walk with a swagger, a dozen or more ways to hurt anyone foolish enough to confront them hanging from their belts. These are not men blessed with a great sense of humor, and I get the feeling that they would like nothing more than another good "collar" and a story to tell their thug cohorts over beers.

A very suspicious Filipino naturalized citizen of the US is the appointed guardian of America's safety and freedom for my lane.

"Citizenship!" he demands.

I hand him my driver's license. He studies it closely, and then looks at me to make sure I look like the picture on the license. I have the fleeting idea of some day donning an Elvis Presley wig when I cross, just to see if he noticed.

"What is the purpose of your trip to Mexico?" he demands, peering suspiciously into the interior of my car.

Immediately I discard the idea of the Elvis wig, and blurt out "Gold! I am bringing gold, but this is all I have, honest!"

He is at once energized, grabs the vial of gold I am holding, and his mind turns immediately to awards and promotions and merit badges if it is discovered that I am indeed a close relative of the Arrellano family of drug dealers, as he suspects. He closes the gate behind me, tells me to turn off the ignition, and calls to secondary on his radio.

Two more armed guards emerge to escort me over to secondary, these not only have side arms, but rifles as well, in case I should try to make a run for it between the gate and secondary. After all, the Golden Gate bridge is a scant 600 miles away, and they have no idea if I have a trunk full of explosives or not. But I don't attempt a break, and am soon doing the perp walk into the interrogation center. While I am being grilled as to where and how I got the gold, my truck is being gone over with a fine-toothed comb, presumably on the theory that if I declared that much gold, surely I had a lot more hidden that I hadn't declared. At the same time, I am being entered into a dozen interrelated computer databases that include the names and profiles of every person who in the past had compromised the security of our country by smuggling, driving too fast, jaywalking or taking that tag off the mattress that you are not supposed to touch.

After much probing and searching, both verbally and electronically, nothing pointing to my involvement in a sinister plot or conspiracy against our country is uncovered. With hopes of citations for valor, vigilance, and exemplary conduct fading, my captors decide to let me go – minus the gold of course. That, I am informed, they will have to keep until its origin and ownership can be determined. If it is awarded to me, a healthy percentage will be deducted as import duty, and I will be taxed heavily on the remainder. All the rest, of course, will be mine to keep.

But all this doesn't happen, because at the border I simply say "I have a bottle of Tequila and a ceramic statue of Jesus".

He says "Go on.", and I do, all the way to Las Vegas, where I sell the gold.

This is the moment of truth! I have in spite of all the potential dangers gotten the gold into the hands of the person that might actually pay me for it! He tells me he has to send it out to be assayed, and will pay me according to how pure the assay says the gold is. Dutifully, I pay for the costs of the assaying process. When I return in two days, the man in the gold broker's office has good news for me. The gold has tested out very well indeed, and he pays me, minus his fee however. At last! After toiling in the desert for weeks, avoiding a phalanx of people who would have loved to separate me from my gold, not to mention breaking multiple laws in two countries, I have good old American dollars in my hand. I thank the man sincerely, and head for the casino.

Oh, how much did I get for my twenty five grams you ask? Well, he gave me....... you know what? It is none of your damned business! I don't know what gold you are talking about.

I Have to Use My Gun

I had been doing a little prospecting and mining in Green Valley one winter, with marginal success. I had done some dry panning, also with mediocre results. There were a few pea sized nuggets, and about two or three ounces of grains that I kept in a little glass vial I always carried for that purpose. In addition, I had found a few quartz outcroppings that had shown some color, and had collected samples to bring back to my house in Bahia de los Angeles for further processing.

As was my habit when I found anything that I wanted to go back to later, I tied some brush on the back end of my truck to hide my tracks until I got to the more well traveled dirt road into wherever I had been. I stopped to untie the brush, and really looked forward to a hot bath and a nice cold beer when I got home, which with no trouble, should be only a couple of hours. As I untied the brush however, I saw another car approaching along the road before me. There were three men in the car, and I watched as they pulled up a few feet away and parked.

When you are alone in the desert, you have to treat anyone you encounter as a potential threat, and in this case I did exactly that. The men got out of their car and walked over to me. All three held beer cans, and I saw from subtle signs that many had preceded the ones they held. They said hello, we talked for a minute, and two of them stepped a few feet away to urinate. The one who remained talking to me seemed like a likeable enough fellow, and he asked me if I would like a cold Bohemia. Well, normally, I would have taken the smart route, declined the offer, gotten back in my car and left on the spot. But, I was so dry, and it had been so long since I had had a cold beer, that my thirst trumped my common sense, and I accepted his offer.

Oh man, that beer was good! We stood and talked for a few minutes, and the one guy offered me a second one, which I also accepted. They were on their way to Calamujue, and we knew some people in common from Bahia de los Angeles. With my guard down, they asked me what I had been doing in the hills, and foolishly I told them. They seemed interested, but not greatly so. I took out the vial of gold to show to the one who had given me the beer. I did this partly because there were only a few ounces in there, and I didn't want them to think I had more than that. He took the vile to look at it, then handed it to one of the others. After both of the others had looked at it, one asked me how much that amount of gold was worth.

"Only about $60 bucks wholesale price." I lied.

I held out my hand to take the vial back, but the man ignored it.

"Chill out old man, I'll give it back." he said, and smiled at me, but his smile didn't reach his eyes. I knew at that point I might be in trouble. The two walked off again to take another leak, and the one with the vial casually put it in his pocket.

That was it for me. I went to the back the truck, pulled my .45 automatic out of my knapsack, and returned to the place we had been talking just as the two walked back. I had the gun in my hand, but did not point it at them. "I want the vial back NOW." I said. "JEEZ", the guy who had given me the beer said, "Give him the damned thing."

For just a moment when he saw the gun, the guy with the vial looked startled, but soon returned to his wise guy smooth talking self.

"Sure, sure, don't get upset old man. I was going to give the damned thing back." He approached me with the vial in his hand. For the first time I pointed the gun at him.

"Put the vial on the ground. Get in your car, and leave."

He slowly and deliberately dropped the vial to the ground, as to mock me, and they all went back to their car, got in, and left. I watched until they disappeared from sight, then picked up the vial and headed for home again. It was all very unnerving to me, as I am by nature not a violent man. When it comes to firearms, I do not want to point one at anyone, or have one pointed at me.

While I drove the short distance to my house, my mind wandered back to a place far away, and an incident that occurred many years ago, but is still very much on my subconscious, and not too far below the surface. It was the first and only time that I have ever killed a man.

As a boatswain's mate in the Navy, I was given a lot of strange duties during my time in the Philippines. Once a buddy of mine and I were assigned a Pilipino soldier who spoke Tagalog, the local language, given a jeep, and told to go find a couple of army deserters who were reportedly in a village nearby. We had their pictures, and the soldier with us would ask any civilians we met if they had seen these guys we were looking for. The situation at that time was very fluid, with the Japanese soldiers retreating to the north, usually in small groups, often isolated, with the American army advancing from two directions.

In our eagerness to find our deserters, we apparently went a little too far, and entered the wrong village. It had not yet been completely abandoned by the Japanese. We had parked the jeep in the center of the village by the well, and split up to continue our search. I rounded the corner of a building, and almost ran into a Japanese soldier carrying his rifle slung over his shoulder. He was as surprised as I was, and turned and ran. I was wearing a sidearm, a Colt .45 automatic. I took it out of the holster as I gave chase. Not knowing any Japanese, I just shouted "Stop", but he didn't even look back. He still had the rifle slung over his shoulder, and I had my pistol in my hand, so I didn't have much to fear. I had almost caught up to him when he veered to his left and scrambled up a steep slope covered with bushes. I lunged and attempted to grab his foot to drag him back down, but missed, and fell myself, sliding down the hill on my stomach a few feet.

He turned, toward me, swung the rifle off his back, and worked the bolt. I felt a little sorry I would have to kill him, and aimed the .45 at his forehead and pulled the trigger. Nothing happened. An electric shock of fear ran up my backbone, as I pulled the trigger again with no effect. Meantime the Japanese soldier pushed the bolt forward, but he had a problem too. The bolt of his rifle had become tangled in the branches of a bush and would not close! He struggled with it again, which gave me a chance to look at my handgun, and I immediately saw the problem. The clip in the handle had not been firmly pushed into place. Using the heel of my palm, I slammed it into place and worked the slide to chamber a round. While I was doing this, the soldier had succeeded in closing the bolt on his rifle, and lifted it to his shoulder. Everything seemed to be happening in slow motion, and I remember being very calm and deliberate as I again pointed the pistol at his forehead and pulled the trigger. This time there was a roar and I felt the kick of the .45 in my hand. My aim had been perfect. A hole appeared in the soldier's forehead, and a reddish spray filled the air behind his head. His rifle went off as he fell backward, and I felt a searing pain in my right leg. A split second had decided whether I would die, or he would, and I had come out on top.

Everything seemed eerily silent for a while, and then villagers started to appear at the scene. They hated the Japanese very much, and were congratulating me, and all seemed very happy that I had killed the young soldier. They cut the leg off my pants and examined my wounds. With one shot the already dead man had managed to inflict four separate wounds. I had had my leg bent, and the bullet went into one side of my thigh, and out the other. It then went completely through the fleshy part of my lower leg as well. My luck had held, as no bones had been in the path of the slug. The local people carried me into a nearby house, where a young woman cleaned and bandaged my wounds.

As we were required, to do, I made note of the dead man's rank and unit insignia. I even found the sad evidence that this was indeed a human with a life like mine – a picture of a kimono clad woman, with some writing in Kanji on the bottom. I suppose that I had killed men before, but in a very impersonal way. It would have been on the ship, with the noise of big guns firing and the acrid smell of cordite in my nose. I didn't have to see their faces, or the pictures of their wives.

One of the natives who had helped me found the spent Japanese bullet that had gone through my leg, and gave it to me as a souvenir. I later threw it away. If some one had to die, I was glad it was him and not me, but I didn't want any souvenirs of the experience. I never had to kill another man.

The Great Las Flores Shoo-fly Gold Robbery

*T*his is a story that took place long before I arrived at Bahia de los Angeles. I heard it from several sources however and there is abundant evidence that it actually took place. The adobe building that served as the jail at Las Flores still stands. It is in the middle of a beautiful flower strewn meadow about 17 kilometers south of town.

Jose "Chuey" Gomez did not look much like a gold robber. He was probably the last person one would choose to fit that role. He never carried a gun, wasn't very big, and really wasn't very smart either. Chuey wouldn't have weighed over 115 pounds with his pockets full of sand. He was a wiry, sun baked little guy standing only about five foot four in his boots, nondescript in every aspect. He had one hat, one belt, and one pair of boots. He also owned two pairs of pants and shirts, which he changed between about every month or so. He had (fortunately) no wife, no family, no friends, no pets, and virtually no possessions. He lived and worked at the San Juan mine in the mountains just south of Bahia de los Angeles. For working in a hole in the ground all day, passing ore up in buckets to the surface, he was paid a small salary. He had no vacation pay, no health insurance, no social security, and was perpetually one accident away from being permanently injured and left on the streets of some Mexican town to fend for himself. As everyone knew and understood, the mines were dangerous places to work.

As with most people though, Chuey did have one activity in which he excelled. It was drinking. One good drag on his bottle of Mescal, and he was on his way to never-never land for the rest of the evening. Every other weekend he would go into Bahia de los Angeles and buy a goodly supply of Mescal, and some tobacco and cigarette papers. In spite of the fact that these items were very cheap, they took the majority of his pay. Sometimes he would have enough money left over to go to the black tent that was pitched on some weekends near the army barracks outside of town. This tent had four makeshift bedrooms, and each was complete with a painted lady of the evening brought all the way from Tijuana to ply her trade. These brave women seemed to have a great tolerance for clients who bathed infrequently, and these visits represented the sole entries on Chuey's social calendar. It was not a great life, but it was good enough for him.

The other miners did not especially like, nor did they dislike Chuey. They expected a good day's work in the mines from him, and this they got. Hung over or not, he always pulled his own weight during the workday. His nightly benders would have been considered relatively normal as well, and tolerated by the other miners, except for one thing. As time went on, Chuey began to augment his income with a little nocturnal redistribution of wealth. He would steal anything that was not nailed down, and could be spent, sold or bartered in town for mescal, tobacco, and the favors of the ladies from Tijuana. Sometimes he got away with it. Sometimes he got caught, and according to the unwritten rules of the mining camp, the offended party was free to show his displeasure by administering a severe beating. They did this with great relish, and Chuey was constantly sporting a shiner, or a cut lip. But, even this did not stop his nighttime raids on other people's property, so it was decided to teach him a lesson once and for all. Chuey would be sent to the carcel at Las Flores. Now, the jail at Las Flores was not too comfortable a place, and it was hoped that Mr. Gomez would once and for all renounce his life of sin after a few days of lost freedom. Then, and only then, could he once more join his fellow workers at the San Juan, presumably and hopefully as a changed man.

Las Flores was the site of the stamp mill on the desert floor at the foot of the mountains. It was where the ore from the San Juan mine was processed. There the gold and high grade ore was extracted from the raw ore sent down from the mine. The "jail" was one half of an adobe single story building. It had a door with a stout lock, and a small window with heavy bars. The daytime temperature rose to well over a hundred degrees in the summer, and the inside of that building was sweltering. It usually was enough of an ordeal to rehabilitate the most hardened of criminals. It was in this room that Chuey was locked, with the proviso that he could leave in one week, if indeed he was still surviving.

It happened to be the case that the jail building was the stoutest structure at Las Flores. It had the thickest and most secure walls. For this reason, the other room was used to store the gold ingots that had been melted down at the smelter. A small, barred window separated the one cell from the gold storeroom. The gold ingots were kept in a wooden box on the far side of the room. It was well out of reach of anyone in the adjacent cell. Chuey settled into his cell to begin his week of incarceration. As his eyes became accustomed to the dim light, he could see through the barred window into the storeroom. He saw the gold ingots in the box on the far side, more gold than he had ever seen.

Now, as we have already noted, Chuey was not the brightest of men, nor blessed with a rich imagination. But he did have two very powerful things going for him. First of all, he had a long time to think about that gold, so tantalizingly close, yet so far out of reach. Secondly, he was keenly aware that even a tiny amount of that glistening yellow metal could get him Mescal, tobacco, and mujeres, which to him were the most important things in life.

A normal person in that situation would have realized that the gold was too far away to reach, and begun to think about more practical things, like staying alive. But not Chuey. He was not smart enough to realize that he couldn't possibly reach those gold ingots, so he sat, and thought, and thought. That evening the chief mining engineer opened the door to the storehouse, counted all the ingots, added some from that day's smeltering, and left. So, the ingots were counted every day. If any were to be found missing, they would not have to look too far to find them.

The next day Chuey tried, and found that he could barely fit his arms between the bars on the small window separating the two rooms, but the gold was still several feet out of reach. So, he sat some more, and thought some more. At last a dim light went off in his brain, and he took off his belt. He had been put in jail with his hat still on, which was a stroke of luck for him, as all the miners of the time had a neck cord attached to their sombreros. The cord was used to keep the hat on while riding horseback, or in a stiff wind. At other times, it was usually worn behind the head, trailing down the wearer's back and thus out of the way. Also typically, this cord had at the bottom a metal clip, commonly known as a 'shoo-fly". The cord and the hat were often used to rid the face of pesky flies so common in the desert, hence the odd name.

Chuey's mind, so rarely used for planning, was now definitely on a roll. For perhaps the first time in his life, he was focusing all of his normally modest mental powers on one goal, and was experiencing a rare moment of astute reasoning. He used the shoo-fly to bore a hole in his belt on the extreme opposite end from the buckle. He removed the shoo-fly cord from his sombrero, and carefully passed one end through the hole and knotted it. He then fashioned a slip-noose out of the other end of the shoo-fly cord, so that like a hangman's knot, it would tighten as it was pulled. He was shaking with excitement as he extended his arm through the bars of the window to the storeroom, holding on to the buckle of the belt. He had to take several minutes to master a technique of swinging the belt like a pendulum, and then flicking it like cracking a whip in the direction of the wooden box holding the gold.

He was elated to see that the string with the noose on the end could indeed reach all the way to the box. The problem was that the belt was much heavier than the cord, and when it passed the top of it's arc and headed down again, it dragged the cord off the box with it. Chuey realized that the only way he was going to get the noose to close around one of the ingots was to get lucky with a toss, and snag one end of the ingot before the belt pulled the cord out of the box and onto the floor. He was facing almost impossible odds, but also had a few things in his favor. First of all, the ingots were shaped sort of like dog biscuits, flared on both ends, and narrower in the middle. Secondly, and very luckily for him, the chief engineer had not stacked the ingots neatly in rows in the box, but had tossed them into a pile in the box. Chuey saw to his delight that a couple of them had one end sticking up out of the pile. Now, if he could just get the noose to fall even partially around one extended end of an ingot, and he pulled very carefully, he might be able to snag it in the noose he had fashioned. It was a long shot, the odds were against him, but on the other hand he had nothing else to do for a few days, and a lot of time to try his luck.

All the rest of the day he tried, and failed, to get the noose to land far enough around one end of an ingot to be able to pull it tight. He came agonizingly close at times, and the cord would be partially around a heavy ingot, but when he pulled it, ever so gently, it slipped off rather than tightening. He finally had to stop trying, as it was getting time for the mining engineer to make the daily addition and tally the total. After the engineer had come and gone, Chuey peeked in and was relieved to see that he had once again just thrown the bars into the box at random, and several of them had one end extending upwards enticingly.

The next morning his arm muscles ached and his shoulder was stiff from the constant awkward action of tossing the noose, but he ignored the pain and started in again. After a multitude of unsuccessful tries that morning, certainly numbering well into the hundreds, a lucky toss partially snagged one end of an ingot. The belt and the cord held taught, in a straight line to the box. Chuey held his breath, and pulled very slowly, but increasingly tightly, the ingot moved slightly, and he felt the noose slip shut. After that, it was just a matter of pulling the cord and dragging the heavy ingot out of the box, and across the floor, up the wall, and through the bars and into his trembling hands. He held a fortune of gold in his hands!

But even in Chuey's normally lightly used brain, there were some nagging doubts. Some vexing problems would have to be solved if this gold was ever truly to be his. Within a few hours, the chief engineer would be in to count the ingots. There was no way he could hide an object as large as a gold ingot in his cell. And what would happen when they found it? He might even be sent to that big carcel in Ensenada, and not for a week, but for years! The elation of actually holding the gold ingot slowly gave way to a fear of what might befall him if he was discovered. As everyone knows, God protects fools and little children, and Chuey, while not young, did fall clearly into one of these two categories. A clever idea came to him, as in a divine inspiration. A VERY clever idea indeed!

He wasted no time putting his plan into action. Taking the metal shoo-fly clip from his hat cord, he used the sharp end of the metal to very, very carefully shave small pieces of gold off of the ingot. He did this very slowly and deliberately, following and maintaining the curves of the ingot, never taking much off any one part, scraping evenly and uniformly. He rubbed the ingot with his thumb, and was very pleased with his work. The ingot was still smooth, had retained it's shape, and the difference was not noticeable in the least. He had obtained a sizeable pile of very thin shavings. The ingots were not weighed each day, they were merely counted. Thus the slight amount missing would not likely be detected until the gold reached its destination far to the north, if it was noticed at all..

The problem still remaining was a formidable one - how to get the ingot back into the box. All he had to do was throw the ingot from his cell, back into the box. This was infinitely easier than the process of extracting it. Easy maybe, but, if he missed......... all was lost. The wooden box was against the far wall of the room, so Chuey decided he would try to hit the wall just above the box, and have the ingot fall into it. He extended his arm through the bars, and straight down, then lifted it up and forward several times in a pendulum action. His touch would have to be just right. No basketball player ever concentrated more on a free throw than Chuey did on that seven foot toss. The Mescal, tobacco, women, everything, depended on the accuracy of this one try. He let the ingot fly, and it hit the wall just above the box, and fell into it among the others. He had done it!

Chuey then set about prying loose a small chunk of adobe brick from the floor of the cell next to one wall. He hollowed out a thimble sized hole under the piece he had removed.

Gathering up the gold shavings, he tore off a piece of his shirt tail, wrapped the gold in it, and put it in the hole he had made under the floor. He then replaced the piece of adobe, and carefully spread sand and dust over the spot until it was undetectable. The gold counter came once again that afternoon, carried out his normal routine, noticed nothing unusual, and left. Chuey could not believe his luck. His plan was working!

For the next five days, the scene was repeated. Each time he was successful at snagging an ingot, and each time he managed to get it back into the box with the slight reduction in size undetected. Twice he had to enlarge his hiding place to accommodate the growing bulk of his gold shavings. On the night before his release, he decided to hide his gold shavings in his inner hat band, and took a lot of time carefully positioning each shaving. The next morning, he was let out as agreed, and told to go back up to the mine. Chuey started out in the direction of the San Juan, but as soon as he was out of sight he changed course and headed for town.

In those days gold was often used for barter, and nobody thought much of this usually poor man having more than usual to spend. After all, everybody gets lucky some times. Chuey had all the Mescal he could possibly drink, and even took to buying the more expensive Tequila at The Diaz Cantina in town. He was sorry it was not yet the weekend that the tent would be pitched by the army barracks. But soon that day did come, and Chuey became their best customer. He soon managed to spend all of gold that he had left. So, there was nothing left to do but to go back up to the mine and try to get his job back. The mine foreman was surprised to see him, as he had been gone longer than expected, but after undergoing a stern lecture and vowing a chastened promise to change his ways, Chuey was allowed to go back to work.

For some reason unknown to his fellow miners however, he suffered a remission of his chronic pilfering, and was again sent to the jail, this time for two weeks. After two weeks in the cell, he left once more, with a light heart and a heavy hatband. This time it took him almost a month to spend his gold, but when he went to get his job back, he was refused. Being thus deprived of his recently adopted way of making a living, he was just about out of ideas. In order to be thrown into the miner's jail, you had to be a miner, and they wouldn't let him work in the mine any more.

Once again a stroke of genius somehow found its way into his usually sluggish mind, and he realized he would have to enroll one of his former fellow miners in his plot. He waited until a man he knew well from the mine, Enrique, came into town. Chuey swore him to secrecy, and outlined his plan. For revealing the secret source of wealth, Chuey wanted half of what Enrique made off with. But sadly, this time his plan did not work. Enrique told Chuey that he would under no circumstances do anything like that! Why, if he got caught, it could be years in the jail in Ensenada! Chuey was crestfallen, but the very next day, he met Francisco, another friend of his in the Cantina. What luck! He again requested, and received, strict confidence from Francisco, before once more making the offer. "You are a very clever man Sr. Gomez!" he said, "But this I could never do, because as you can see my arms are much larger than yours, and would never fit between the bars. Besides, I am not a good thrower, and would probably miss the wooden box and wind up in the carcel in Ensenada."

At this point, Chuey was out of ideas, and had to give up hope of ever getting into the jail again. He found work as a fisherman on a panga out of Calamujue, and nobody ever saw him in Bahia again. The following week, both Enrique and Francisco became uncharacteristically belligerent, and both wound up in the little jail. Shortly after they were released, Rafael and Faustino both committed offenses and were sent to the jail. The mine foreman wondered what on earth had gotten into his men. Enrique and Francisco both had asked for their jobs back, only to get thrown into the jail again shortly after Rafael and Faustino had been released.

But, as the saying goes, all good things must come to an end. One day the chief engineer noticed that some of the ingots that had been in the box for a while appeared to be shrinking. He compared them with the newly smelted ones, and immediately detected a difference. Coincidentally, shortly after his discovery of the theft, a rider was arrived from the company office in Mexicali complaining that some of the ingots being sent were underweight. The current prisoners were searched, hatbands and all, and the mystery of the disappearing gold was solved. The company decided to send any further prisoners to the jail in Guerrero Negro, where it was hoped that the prisoners would be more interested in getting out of jail, rather than into it! Thus, what probably was the most popular jail cell in the history of Baja California was closed forever.

Salsipuedes Canyon

$\mathcal{T}$ he vast majority of the time I spent in the desert I was alone. I preferred to be by myself for several reasons. Toward the end of my time spent in the wilds of Baja, would never take anyone with me if I was going to do serious prospecting. My experience in Salsipuedes illustrates one of the major drawbacks to depending on others when times get tough.

Salsipuedes had always been a place I wanted to take a closer look at. The center part of the canyon is extremely inaccessible, and I had never prospected it. The areas nearby that I had been able to get my truck into, and a days walk further in here and there, had paid off in some good finds for me in the past. I had taken out several pretty good nuggets over the years, and was very interested in seeing what lay in the interior of the canyon. The lure of the unknown has always been very strong draw to me.

One very pleasant winter day in Bahia de los Angeles, I sat down with my friend and fellow prospector Rico, and we planned out a trek into the heart of the canyon. Neither of us had ever been there before. We studied the map carefully, noting the distances and the terrain we would have to cross. The scheme we devised was unique in my experience. We decided that we would drive in as far as we could get on the west end of the canyon. Our calculations indicated that we could proceed eastward through the canyon, and come out on the coast of the Sea of Cortez in five days. That was perfect timing, as five days was about the maximum time our supplies would last. We would have to carry in everything we needed on our backs.

Rico's son, Rico Jr., had a panga which he used occasionally for fishing or taking visitors to the islands. Rico said he would give him 45 gallons of gasoline, and arrange for him to pick up after we had been gone five days. A small bay where we would arrive at the coast was selected for the rendezvous.

As we sat studying our maps, Louie, a man we both knew from town drove up. He asked what we were doing, and when he heard of our intentions, he very enthusiastically begged to be able to go along. I think in retrospect that had Rico or I had our choice at the time, we would have declined his request. But Louie was in his early 50's, and looked to be in good shape. Neither of us knew him very well, but lacking any valid reason for refusing, we agreed to include him in our project.

All the preparations were made. We carefully packed our backpacks with all that we would be needing, which was considerable. There were the tools for prospecting and taking samples of ore, food, water, bedding and dozens of odds and ends that had to fit into our load somehow.

At last all was ready, and early one morning we met at my house before daylight and loaded everything into my old truck. Louie showed up with some of his friends. There were four or five of them, some of whom I didn't recognize. They agreed to take us as far as we could go with the vehicles, and then return my truck to town.

By mid-morning we had penetrated the beginnings of the canyon as far as was possible by vehicle. The steep walls of a plateau blocked any further access, and our first task was to climb to the top. I was very pleasantly surprised when three of Louie's friends volunteered to carry our 40 pound backpacks to the top of the plateau for us! At least we would start our hike fresh and full of energy. They all scrambled down the cliff again, and we watched them drive off in the trucks. Heading east across the plateau, we started our adventure.

All went well that first day. We found a very beautiful palm canyon and made camp. There was standing water in a rocky pool at the base of the tall palms. As was my habit in such situations, rather than take the water directly from the pool, I scooped out a hole in the sand near the edge of the pool, and then let water seep into it. I would then take my drinking water out of this little hole, secure in the knowledge that the sand through which it had seeped would have filtered and purified it somewhat. At least that was my theory. Another trick I used frequently to disguise muddy or murky water was to use it to make coffee. It gave all the life-giving moisture needed, but the foul taste would be greatly diminished by the flavor of the coffee.

That evening I did a little prospecting around the campsite, but found nothing of interest. It was winter, and got very cool at night. We cooked our supper over an open fire, then passed around a bottle of tequila and talked of the days to come. When we turned in, the blankets felt good in the crisp and chilly night air.

We were up early the next morning, and the coffee tasted almost as good as the tequila had the night before. In the desert, alcohol has always been my drug of choice in the evening and caffeine in the morning. Hey, it works for me, and a lot of others I know!

Continuing over the relatively level ground, we could see in the distance that there was yet another sharp rise ahead, and an even higher plateau. We reached the face of the cliffs at twilight of the short winter day, and decided to establish a dry camp there, and make our ascent in the morning. The nightly ritual of the supper, tequila, talk, and snug bed was repeated. We awoke refreshed and up to the challenge of scaling the cliffs with our heavy backpacks. I calculated that this higher level must have been around a thousand meters above sea level. There were far fewer of the desert plants that grew so profusely at the lower levels.

The prospecting, on the other hand, was extremely promising. I found several areas that showed good color, and I made notes as to each location. Since we were on foot, and carrying heavy loads, I was precluded from taking samples with me. These days all I would have to do is enter the GPS points, and that would be that. At that time however, I had to rely on my notes, my memory, and sometimes luck, to rediscover the exact spots I had prospected. Louie had proven to be a good hiker, and to this point had been no problem for Rico and me. Now I wanted to spend time investigating ore samples, and he was anxious to continue the hike. I am sure Rico felt the same way. After all, we were not there to take a nice walk through the desert. We were there to look for gold, and that is what we intended to do, whether it irked Louie or not. So, we both ignored his obvious impatience, and took our time doing what we had come to do.

Rico was a pretty good prospector. He had a knack for finding interesting animal trails that often led to areas ripe for prospecting. He was the right mix of independence and cooperation, and I was glad he was along. We spent that day prospecting the area carefully, and we both felt it would be worthwhile to come back and do some digging and processing of ore sometime in the future. It was our second day with no new water, but we had some left, and were not concerned. We felt sure that there would be more palm canyons and water ahead.

As you know by now, I myself had yet another reason to be in Salsipuedes – the Jesuit gold! Anyone who has traversed the dry sands of the central Baja and finally come upon one of the many palm canyons knows the feeling they give. To me, they are beautiful beyond description, and I have spent many a time comfortably camped in their shade and beauty. These palms are not native to the Baja. They were all brought from the mainland, mostly by the Jesuits during their century long stay on this remote peninsula. So, the Jesuits had been here, and everywhere there are palms, which made these areas of particular interest to me in my search. The Indians, the soldiers, and the priests surely frequented these oases, and might well have left some things behind. I intended to look carefully for whatever clues might lie close to any such places we would find.

This highest plateau, while ripe for further prospecting, was dry, and almost lifeless. The next morning, much to Louie's approval, we finished our search for ore and continued across the high plateau. Nightfall overtook us when we were only an hour or two from the eastern edge of the plateau. We made our third dry camp that night, and our water supply diminished even further. Surely some palm canyons with water lay somewhere before us, at the lower levels. We were still not overly concerned about water.

When we reached the eastern edge of the mesa, we were greeted with a very beautiful and encouraging view. Below us, we saw clearly the sparkling blue water of the gulf. Directly ahead we could see the bay where our rendezvous with the panga was to take place the following day. Even better, there was a small group of palm trees that could be seen in a rocky ravine about half way to the coast. Since our water supply was getting low, we headed straight for it, arriving in the afternoon.

We were disappointed to find that upon entering the palm shaded ravine, there was no standing water to be found. Rico and I immediately began digging in the sand close to one of the taller palms. Both of us knew that almost always there would be water to be found below the surface in such areas. This turned out to be one of the exceptions to the rule however, and no matter how deep, or where we dug, we found no water. This was a rather serious surprise.

It was decided that we would immediately begin rationing our water, and pool our supply. Up to that point, we had been each carrying our own water, and drinking according to our own needs. We selected one container, and Rico and I both poured our remaining water into it. Louie showed us his container – it was almost empty, only a swallow left, so we let him drink it then and there. The situation was more uncomfortable than dangerous, as we would arrive at the designated meeting point on the coast the next day, and Rico Jr. would be sure to have water with him. Even if he didn't, Bahia de los Angeles was less than three hours away by boat.

Nature had other plans in store for us however. Later that night, a brisk wind began to blow. In a matter of minutes, it increased in intensity until it was fairly howling around us, as sometimes happens in that part of the Baja. We just crawled further into our bedding and drew the blankets tightly around us lest they blow away into the night.

When daylight came, the winds were unabated. It was impossible to make a fire or to cook anything for breakfast, so we just packed up quickly and made for the coast. We arrived at the bay after stumbling through the stormy blasts of wind, and looked for a moment at the whitecaps and turbulence in the water. There would be no boats venturing out from Bahia that day, we knew. No pangero would be foolhardy enough to challenge the gulf in one of its angry moods. We found a somewhat sheltered spot among some rocks and settled in to wait. Our little camp afforded us a good view of the rocky points on either side of the little bay, and we began watching for something we knew would not be seen that day.

There was no change in the velocity of the wind on the next day. We were now almost completely out of water. We calculated that we had enough for one swallow apiece in the morning and another in the evening. Watching and waiting, another day passed, and now our water was completely exhausted. We had been gone for six days now, and still had hope that rescue would be imminent. The seventh day, the winds seemed to have lessened somewhat, but the waves still pounded the rocky shore with vengeance, and surely would have smashed any panga foolish enough to try to enter the bay.

That night Rico told me that he thought we should leave this bay, and head for the one directly to the south. He knew it well. It was broader, and had sandy patches of beach much safer for a boat to put ashore. The plan seemed ok to me. On one hand, I was reluctant to leave the place we had agreed to meet. But, since we would be heading south, whoever came after us would have to pass by that bay as well, and would see us on the shore. I agreed, and the next morning we left, with no water at all. It was impossible to follow the coastline, as the bays are separated by almost sheer rock faces which extend all the way into the water. The only way to reach the cove to the south was to go directly back up the cliff we had come down, follow the ridge south, then descend again on the other side of the point.

Rico had been right. This beach was much more open, and would be an easy place for a panga to land in calm weather. But, the weather was still far from calm. We spent our third day without water. I am convinced that the only thing that kept us alive was the fact that it was the middle of the winter, and we did not lose a lot of water through sweating. There were no succulent plants anywhere in the little area around the bay, which like the first one was surrounded by almost vertical cliffs. By the morning of the fourth day without water however, our situation was becoming serious indeed. Near the northern point of the bay were three graves, marked with metal crosses. They gave the place its name "Punta Mortuaria", or Mortuary Point. It seemed very fitting to us, and we speculated whether or not there would be three more graves there one day soon!

Rico, for one, had not lost his sense of humor. I decided that day to turn my knapsack inside out to find any tidbit that might have been lost in the bottom. To my delight, I discovered three long overlooked cough drops in the bottom of one pocket. I gave one to Louie, one to Rico, and kept one for myself. "Well amigo", Rico said to me when I gave him the cough drop, "At least if we are going to die, we will die healthy!"

The wind continued to blow. I hallucinated that nature had gone berserk, that this wind would last forever, that wind would be eternal, and calmness would never come. Rico said that maybe we should go back to the palm canyon, and dig a little further down, or in some other place, and that maybe we would find water. Louie agreed with him, saying he would remain behind in case the boat came while we were gone. I didn't like the idea at all, and argued against it on the grounds that we might not find any water, and that would dissipate what energy we had left, and we would surely die. Our best bet was to stay put, and hope for the wind to end. At last I managed to persuade Rico, and he gave up the idea.

Later that morning we were lying in our blankets, the sky was covered with dark clouds and the wind continued unabated. I saw Rico sit up suddenly, and cock his head to one side. I sat up too and said

"What...."

"Shhhhhhhhhhhh" he held up his hand to quiet me.

After a few seconds of straining to hear through the wind, I thought I too heard something. At first I couldn't make out what it was, it sounded like a series of low pitched thuds. As the sound grew very gradually louder, I recognized it with unbounded joy and relief. It was now an unmistakable sound, the chug chug chug chug of a diesel engine. Surely it was not Rico Jr., as his panga had a two-stroke outboard which made a completely different sound. The noise grew louder, and bounced off the rock walls of the northern edge of the cove, but still nothing was in sight. A few seconds later, the bow of a very large boat nosed around the point. As it hove into view, we all recognized it immediately as the largest vessel in Bahia de los Angeles. It belonged to a man we knew well, Gilbert, an American who lived south of town. We danced on the beach, waved arms, and yelled ineffectively against the noise of the wind.

The fifty foot vessel came to a stop and dropped anchor. A small boat was put in the water, and headed toward us. At that moment, something happened that I will never forget – and became one of the reasons I preferred to risk nature alone rather than to depend on other people. Louie came up with a broad smile on his face. "Hey fellas, let's finish this!" He held up a quart sized plastic bottle about half full of water. "I was saving this for our reserve."

I think the only thing that saved Louie's life at that moment was that the dinghy was getting close, and if we had killed him, as we both dearly wished to do, there would have been witnesses. There are not a lot of things a man can do to me that would cause me to despise him the way I despised Louie from that day on – and in fact to this day.

Gilbert said that Rico Jr. had sold the gasoline for beer money, and had been trying to get some one to come and get us, on the theory that "My dad will pay you." but hadn't been able to convince anyone. Finally, Gilbert, good man that he was, had decided to brave the weather and go look for us. He had no idea that we would be out of water.

The story got spread around Bahia about what Louie had done, and things got so bad that he finally sold his house and moved back to California. Good riddance, pinche cabron! Oh, and one last thing. Remember the name of the Canyon we were in, "Salsipuedes"? Well, in Spanish "Sal si puedes" means "Leave, or get out – if – you are able." No place could have been more aptly named.

I Meet One *Tough* Goat

CHAPTER 26

One time I was prospecting on a mountain ridge west of Yubay, and had set up camp in a remote but beautiful spot. It was accessible enough so that I could drive all the way there in my old truck. The clearing I chose was surrounded by big rocks and smoke trees, cardon, and ocotillo, and made a comfortable camp indeed. After I had been there a few days, I was getting tired of eating my canned goods and tortillas. One morning I woke to hear sounds coming from near my truck. I saw it was an old male mountain goat with his front feet on the fender of my truck, his head stuck in my supplies that were in the bed. He was rooting around in my food supply, looking for something to eat. I shouted at him, and goats being as wary of humans as they are, I expected him to take off at top speed as soon as he saw me. Instead, he just stopped his searching for edibles, and turned to eye me suspiciously. Damn! This was an unusual goat. I got up, picked up a rock and threw it at him. This got his attention, and he reluctantly fled the scene.

I didn't think much more about it, until that night when I again selected supper from my dwindling supply of canned goods. Wow, it would be good to have some nice meat with my beans and rice. I thought about the mountain goat, and his strange behavior. It dawned on me that he might have been so bold because he was growing old and feeble, and it was harder and harder for him to get enough to eat. He was alone too, and so hungry that my shouts had not been enough to evict him from my truck. I had seen this in other animals many times in the desert. It is the animal who is deprived of his normal forage that, by dint of necessity, is willing to take the most risks. Not only would a little goat meat be a great improvement to my menu selection, but I rationalized that the poor critter would be meat for the Zopilotes, the turkey vultures, very soon if he didn't wind in my pan first. I resolved to put the poor beast out of his misery if we met again, and that night slept with my .22 rifle at my side.

The next morning, sure enough, his hunger again overcame his innate sense of caution, and for the second day I was awakened by the sound of him rifling through my truck bed. Slowly and quietly I worked the bolt action on my rifle, took aim, being careful to miss my dependable old truck, and squeezed the trigger. The crack of the rifle in the dark of dawn echoed off the nearby cliffs, and a fountain of sparks and fire spewed forth from the rifle barrel. I looked, and the goat was no longer visible over the bed of my truck. I got up and ran over to the truck, and saw the goat running away on the other side. I ran a few steps after him, hoping to get anther shot, but not having much of a chance of hitting him from this distance, as I had just missed from much closer. And then, I swear, as unlikely as it seems, that goat stopped, and turned around and looked at me. As I watched not being able to believe what I was seeing, he started running directly toward me at what must have been his top speed. I shot and missed, and he kept coming. I was starting to feel a little more apprehensive with each split second of his approach. Yes, he was old, and yes, I did have a gun.

On the other hand, the goat had a lot going for him too. He was desperate and desperate people OR animals are always best avoided. In addition, HE had the horns, I didn't. He had the momentum, I was standing still. And most ominous of all, I had already fired twice and missed him both times. I had visions of becoming the butt of a story that would be told around many a campfire for years to come. "You remember old Herman Hill?" it would start. "Well, believe it or not, he was found next to his pickup, killed by a goat!" My progeny for generations would carry my shame on their backs like an albatross. The name of Herman Hill would be sneered, rather than spoken.

The specter of such a fate made me summon more courage, and I stood my ground. I fired a third time when he was about thirty feet away, and this time, I did manage to hit him at the base of one horn. It in no way deterred him or impeded his progress however, and he continued straight for me at unabated speed and perfect accuracy of attack. From this point on, my higher order thinking skills were no longer in control. All those powers of logic and abstract reasoning that had raised my species over his were superseded by the primitive imperative for survival. I turned, raced for the truck and launched myself the last few feet by air into the bed of the truck. I hit the truck bed about the same time the goat hit the side of my truck with a tremendous crash that shook the vehicle violently..

Then all was silence, as I lay there, my limbs reporting in to my brain as to injuries I might have sustained in my leap and subsequent collision with the truck bed, but there were none. I cautiously got to my knees, and looked over the side where the collision had taken place. There lay the goat, almost peacefully, dead with his head bent at an impossible angle. There was a large dent in the fender. What I had been unable to do; my beloved and faithful truck had done for me.

I thought of just burying the goat, as the dignity of his bravery demanded, but the thought of savory roasting meat won out. I spent the morning butchering the carcass and preparing the meat. Some I cooked, and some I prepared as jerky, that would last me for days if not weeks. Not a bit of that valiant creature went to waste. Some savage tribes think that if you eat your foe, you will gain his strength. I kind of hoped that was true, because I did have a healthy respect for the old fellow's courage and daring. Besides, with rice and beans, he was delicious.

The rest of that trip, I debated between having a good story to tell, and coming off a little like a pinche gringo, or just to forget the whole thing and keep my mouth shut. Now you know what I chose! It was just too good of a story to keep to myself.

My Mexican "Partner"

CHAPTER 27

It never ceases to amaze me how misunderstood the realities of prospecting and mining are to the average person. Sometimes I think that the only way to really understand prospecting, is to do it for a period of time. People's attitude toward mining is somewhat predictable. Most think that it is easy. All you have to do is go into the desert, find the gold, get it out of the rock it is in, bring it back and sell it. "Just show me how to do it, that is all I ask", is something I have heard a lot of times. It is a little bit like going up to Andres Segovia and saying "Wow, I really like that music. I have an hour or two, show me how to play that thing." Finding gold, being an art like music or painting, is not a matter of just "doing it." To do it well takes years of practice, talent, and determination to excel. Nor does anyone say, "I am interested in the stars, show me how to be an astronomer." Like astronomy, prospecting is also a science. The astronomer must be well versed in math and physics to make sense of what he sees. The prospector must know applied geology and chemistry to find and extract the gold.

An incident that occurred to me some years ago is a good illustration of this lack of understanding on the part of would-be prospectors. I had been working an area in the mountains above Bahia de los Angeles for a month, and was about ready to wind up my trip. I was tired, as I had been laboring long hours, from dawn till dusk daily, and had only managed to average about ten or fifteen grams of gold per day. It was hard work and the rewards had been meager. I was ready for a shower and a clean set of clothes, so I decided to pack up and head for home.

It was early in December as I hiked to my truck and drove down the canyon roads descending toward Bahia de los Angeles. The winter air was clear and cool. I saw the beautiful blue waters of the Sea of Cortez far below me, always a welcome sight. I looked forward greatly to a couple of weeks of rest before I traveled north for Christmas. True, I had not found a lot of gold, but it would be enough for a well deserved vacation. After a couple of weeks of rest in town, I planned to take my poke up to Las Vegas, cash it in, and spend the holiday season with my friends and family in Nevada. The thought of spending time in an air-conditioned casino with mini-skirted Keno girls bringing me drinks was much on my mind.

One morning when I had been home no more than a couple of days, as I sat on my front porch enjoying a cold Pacifico, a friend from town came by.

"Hola Jesus. Que paso?" I greeted him.

"Oh Senor Herman, I am well, but very sad. Christmas is coming soon, and I have no money to buy presents for my family. You know how to find gold in the mountains, and I thought perhaps you could take me with you, and show me how I too could find some gold."

"Well, Jesus, it is very hard to find the gold. I have worked all day long, and only found about fifteen grams or so a day, and I have been panning for years. You would have to learn, so it would be very difficult for both of us to get even a couple of grams a day."

I went to get him a cold Pacifico. He reflected gravely for a few moments, then asked, "Senor Herman, how much money do you think we would get for the gold, you and I together, if you show me how to do it?"

"Oh, it varies, but I think maybe about 20 grams a day between the two of us," I said.

His face brightened, "I could buy many presents for my family with that much gold! They would be very happy, and Christmas for me would be good!"

I was torn between insisting on my well deserved rest before my trip north, and helping Jesus and his family. After a few moments reflection, I decided maybe I could throw some food in the truck, and go back up to the mountains to see if we could find a little more gold for this poor man's family to help the holidays.

"Ok Jesus, we will go for one week. But I warn you, it is very hard work, and there may be very little gold."

He leaped to his feet, pumping my hand vigorously,

"Oh Senor Herman, thank you! I will be ready to go tomorrow morning!" He turned to leave, then hesitated, and said "Oh, Senor Herman, there is one more thing......"

"Yes, Jesus, what is it?"

Is it possible that you could pay me now for the gold we will find?" At that moment, I knew that he had no idea what gold prospecting was all about. To him it was sort of a salary that the desert paid if you worked hard enough, automatic, dependable, and predictable. This man would never forgive me if we went out to the desert and found no gold. He would think I had cheated him, and was refusing to "show him how to do it."

Needless to say, he did not become my prospecting partner, and I was able to enjoy my rest after all. I did go to Las Vegas, and did damned well at the Roulette tables. But, that is another story!

The Tailings at Las Flores

$\mathcal{T}$ his is a story that took place shortly after I arrived in Bahia de los Angeles. The leached and now presumably worthless rock still lies unwanted on the desert floor at Las Flores, having twice bestowed its hidden treasure. The only other thing that remains is the story, which has often been told, and probably will continue to be told for many years to come.

For decades the tailings, pulverized rock left over from the gold extraction processing of the original ore, lay on the desert floor like a series of modern day pyramids. Las Flores is only a short distance south of the town of Bahia de los Angeles, and very accessible by road. These man-made hills of sand and gravel lay untouched, for decades serving only as a slightly ugly blight on an otherwise beautiful desert scene. After all, what was more useless than rock from which all the gold had been taken, right? Wrong! As time went on, two things happened to kindle renewed interest in those sun baked piles of ground up rock.

One was a steady advance in the technology of gold extraction. The mills at San Juan had been as good as any for their time, and they got most of the gold out of the ore, but not all of it. What they had missed was still there, in all the thousands of tons of tailings piled conveniently, waiting for some one to free it. It is estimated that the original milling process removed around 80% of the gold that the ore actually held, but modern methods could get more than 90%. That meant that about 10% of the gold that nature had put in those rocks was still there. The San Juan mine had been one of the best producing gold mines in all of Baja, and even ten percent of what it had produced would be worth a lot of money. The other factor was that the price of gold was rising fast. It was only a matter of time before some one came to rework the tailings.

The first to cash in on the potential of the tailings was Antero Diaz, the founding father of the modern town of Bahia de los Angeles. He sold the rights to a group from Ensenada. This group arrived at exactly the same time as a second group, who had also been sold the rights to the ore. This contingent had bought the tailings not from Diaz, but from the president of the Ejido Libertad Y Tierra, which owned the land. Needless to say, there was a great deal of confusion as to whom the right to process the ore actually belonged. Both groups had impressively legal appearing paperwork granting them the right, and both had paid the agreed amount. The Diaz family argued that they had retained the mineral rights to the land, and of course, the ejido claimed them as well. Both groups of miners established camps near the tailings, as the haggling over ownership went on longer and longer. At length, the two camps grew restless and attempted to persuade the other to leave. They both employed the same simple, but time proven tactic. They bashed as many heads and broke as many bones of their adversaries as they could.

The town Delegado and his hastily enlisted group of deputized local residents kept order as well as they could, but their efforts were not equal to the task at hand. The nightly mayhem continued unabated. Finally, it was decided to build a fence between the two groups, and station a guard at both ends. This idea worked, but due more to the fact that most of the miners had grown tired of waiting and returned north to their homes. Finally, those who remained ran out of money for buying beer in town, and they left as well, returning the site once again to it's normal peaceful existence. No money was returned, and eventually, after many years of litigation, it was decided that the Ejido did indeed have the rights to the now infamous rock pile.

By this time, the state of the art of extracting gold from ore had greatly advanced, especially from ore milled as long ago as this had been. A method was discovered and begun to be used throughout the mining industry that used cyanide to leach out the gold. It was extremely efficient, and used correctly could remove almost all the gold from finely milled ore. The President of the Ejido selected a Dentist from Los Angeles and again sold the rights to the project. The dentist was a good candidate, as he had worked with gold through his profession, and was well aware of all the modern chemical methods for its efficient extraction. Also helpful was the fact that he had a wife that was a Mexican citizen and spoke perfect Spanish. Most importantly of all, he had the cash.

He came to town shortly after he had gained the rights, and I struck up a conversation with him over dinner at Guillermo's restaurant. After dinner, we went into the bar, and when he learned of my background in mining, and my familiarity with the chemical processes for gold extraction, he offered me a job on the spot. I was reluctant to work for anyone else, as it had been my lifelong habit to be my own boss, so I turned him down. I did offer to give what advice I could, and consult on the various phases of the project. On that basis we finally struck a deal, and agreed to work together. The first thing we did was to sit down and calculate exactly what equipment, materials, and supplies would be needed. I was able to tell him what ratio of cyanide to water that should be used. My estimate turned out to be right on the money, and we never did change it.

A few months later, when all the equipment had arrived, we began the mammoth undertaking. We started by laying out giant tarps on the ground. They had been custom made in the US to our specifications, and had cost the dentist a fortune, but not as big a fortune by far as the one we hoped it would help us accrue. We began mixing the tailings with powdered sulfur, which was needed to restrict and control the action of the very powerful cyanide, When we had a mixture of several hundred tons on the tarp, we rigged a sprinkling system over the top to release the water and cyanide mixture onto the ore. This was a painstaking and arduous task, but it was essential that it be done correctly, so we took our time, checking and rechecking every step. The liquid mixture had to seep slowly into the pile, and dampen the ore evenly and thoroughly. Using too much of the solution would overpower the sulfur and make the job of extracting the gold at the end of the process much harder.

Finally, the day arrived when we were ready to begin. We started the slow water flow, and waited. It worked perfectly, the cyanide laced water seeped slowly through the rock, soaking it uniformly, reacting with the sulfur and absorbing the particles of gold, passing down onto the tarp below. The tarp had been situated so that it was slightly lower at one end. We had designed and installed three drains into the lower side of the tarp. The drains emptied into 55 gallon metal drums. At last, the liquid began to flow, and was caught in the holding tanks. Once each tank was filled, it was replaced with an empty one, and set aside to settle. A residue eventually collected at the bottom, the water and cyanide was poured off, and the remaining gold-bearing muck was drawn off into a smaller vessel. Now all that remained was to precipitate out the gold. I soon found that the dentist himself was the only one who was allowed to perform this last operation. It was only then that it could be determined exactly how much gold had been extracted, and he was adamant that he, and only he, would be the one to perform this procedure. So, this last critical operation was carried out in the privacy of his own rented home, and in the presence of only the dentist and his wife.

From my experience, it seemed to me that we had to be gaining a considerable amount of gold from the process. My supposition was bolstered by the fact that the dentist remained very enthusiastic and energetic throughout the course of the proceedings, and maintained the secrecy of exactly what our output of gold amounted to. I really didn't care beyond curiosity, because I had agreed to a fixed price for my services, and didn't care to be involved any further. This was not true of the ejido however, and their increasing demands for an accounting and oversight of the gold being taken began to become a real problem. Presumably the dentist and the representative of the ejido had some sort of a side deal which served as an incentive to keep the production going, because he employed every delaying tactic he could think of to keep the restless and demanding ejido members at bay. Time went on, and the unworked pile of tailings diminished. The dentist's wife made regular trips to her family home in Tijuana. There were those skeptics who thought the springs on her car looked a little low in back. A rather small amount of gold was turned over to the ejido at regular intervals, which still had no way of knowing exactly what percentage of the total take it represented.

Finally the dispute came to a head, and the ejido members voted to shut the project down if an open and honest accounting of the gold was not made. The dentist had no choice but to agree. He said he had all the records, and would submit the entire accounting, since day one of the operation, at the next ejido meeting. The members met the next Sunday, anxious to see the accounting. The dentist did not show up. Some one was dispatched to his house to fetch him, but reported back that he was gone, along with his car, his truck, and some of the refining equipment.

The dentist and his wife were never to be seen in Bahia de los Angeles again. The outrage of the townspeople was somewhat mitigated by the fact that he had left behind a lot of relatively new and expensive equipment. There were tractors, skip loaders, conveyers, irrigation equipment and the like that could be used or sold. The ejido members decided to sell most of the equipment immediately, and split the proceeds between them. Even this slight advantage disappeared when within days people from Ensenada and Tijuana began showing up with valid receipts and bills of sale for all the equipment! The dentist had sold everything weeks before he left, and had given the buyers a date to pick up the equipment after he knew he would already have left!

As one might suspect, neither the Dentist nor his wife has ever returned to the town of Bahia de los Angeles. There are many who live there who would be very anxious to meet them again!

Back To El Desengano

*O*ver the next few years I went back to Mesa Colorada many times. Each time I widened the circle I had originally drawn. I found plenty of gold, sometimes more than others, but never another trace of the Jesuit statuary. I began to question my theory, and to even despair of ever finding another clue. I reminded myself that the desert is so vast, what I was looking for was much less likely to found than the proverbial needle in a haystack. This was a TINY needle, and I was looking in a HUGE haystack. The chances of discovering even what I had found already were against the odds, and I knew that. But I HAD found some things, and I felt they were irrefutable evidence that my theory was correct. I was beginning to lose confidence, but not conviction. In my heart I knew it was out there somewhere, and if anybody could find it, it would be me.

I decided to go back to the spot where I had found the candlestick and gun barrel, and search around them to see if I could turn up any more clues I might have overlooked. Accordingly, I set off one day on a trip back into the beautiful Sierra La Primavera. I passed through the valley where the drug drop had occurred, hoping I wouldn't be involved in anything like that again. I easily located the spot where I had dug originally, and made camp nearby. I spent quite a bit of time digging in and around the same place I had made the earlier find, but uncovered no new clues. After the better part of two days looking in the local vicinity, and running my metal detector over every likely spot, I had turned up nothing new. Finally I was convinced that I had found whatever had been left there, and there was no more to be done. I took a couple of days to prospect the surrounding area before heading north to check out Desengano again.

It was late spring, and the desert was blooming as it always did after the brief but heavy rains that we had enjoyed in March and April. All the animals that loved to eat the lush green grasses that appear so briefly in the desert were in their glory. There were rabbits everywhere.

The next morning I broke camp and headed for Desengano once again. I planned to return to the site where I had found the burro bones, and the empty hole with the bits of rusty metal and rotting leather. It was impossible to get the truck close enough to a suitable campsite, so I had to pack all my things in by foot. It took me the whole rest of the day and evening to take three or four trips back and forth, until the camp was completely ready to be used. I was in the midst of making my dinner, when I saw a real desert drama take place. In the brush at the edge of the clearing I had made camp, I saw a *Correcamino* – a road runner bird, fluttering its wings, rising a few feet up off the ground, and then diving down again. He did this repeatedly. Curious, I took a few steps closer to see what was happening. To my surprise, I saw a good sized *cascabel* – desert rattlesnake, very much under attack by the bird. The snake was trying to defend itself, and get away into the bushes at the same time. But the bird would have none of it. He repeatedly dived in and pecked the snake on the back of the head, and flew out of reach again before the rattler could coil and strike. This went on for some time, and as it did, the snake began to react more and more slowly. As the rattler's ability to defend itself waned, the bird's attacks increased in daring, to the point that the he stood over the snake and pecked without flying away between attacks. Finally the snake lay quietly, and the roadrunner ceased his pecking. He walked around the dead snake for some minutes, and then ran away through the brush. He did not kill the bird to eat it; I guess he just didn't like rattlesnakes. I thought maybe since he usually built his nests on the ground the bird might be getting back for some stolen eggs in the past. Whatever the reason, I was glad the snake was dead. He was too close to my camp for comfort. Such dramas do occur regularly in the desert, and sometimes if you are lucky enough and observant enough, you can be a witness to them. I have always liked the roadrunners, and they are said to bring good luck. Better luck than the rattlers I guess.

I spent the next morning running my metal detector over the big pit in which I had found the burro bones, and the smaller one that had been empty except for the rotting leather. I could get no sign of metal from either one. I searched the whole area around the clearing with my detector, and found nothing. There was little left that I could do at the spot, but before I left I elected to dig a little further down in both places. I dug out the larger pit another two or three feet in depth to no avail. For the smaller one, I decided to forgo the shovel, and dig by hand. I began taking out handfuls of sand and pebbles, when I came across another scrap of decaying leather. Turning it over, I saw what I had been looking for! In an instant, I knew that my theory of the gold, all the years of thinking, planning, guessing - they had been right after all. What I saw was a piece of hammered gold foil about half the size of a fingernail. Hammered gold! It could only have come from an object covered with gold foil, such as many of the relics which once adorned the altar of the church at San Borja had been.

I was glad no one was around to see me, sitting there out in the middle of the desert by myself, laughing out loud like a crazy man. A ton of pent up frustration left me as I joyously held that piece of leather with the tiny bit of gold foil. Damn! I was right! I am going to find it, I promised myself. I drove home the next day a new and re-energized man, anxious to get back to my maps, and try again.

By the Wonderful Waters of Yubay

CHAPTER 30

$\mathcal{O}$f all the sights there are to see in the Baja, for my money some of the most beautiful are the palm canyons one finds at remote places in the mountains. These wonderful spots are perfect shelters from the hot sun and scorching sands of the desert. The shade of the tall palms and the cool water often found beneath them provide a very welcome, and at times life-giving, respite from the rigors of travel in the Baja. Of these, without doubt my favorite is the oasis of Yubay. It is very special to me not only because it is beautiful, and has afforded me much comfort over the years, nor because of its rich heritage and the role it has played in the history of the central Baja. It was near this place that I almost lost my life in a fall from a cliff. Yet, I still love the place dearly, and the primary reason is that it was near here that I came full circle on my theory of, and search for, the Jesuit gold.

I had opted to search an area north of Yubay, the exact location of which shall be omitted here. For reasons stated previously, I intended to scour the area for signs of the Jesuit travelers. I had been in the area many times before, but had mainly been seeking good ore, as I did not believe Yubay lay in the path that the escaping party had taken north from San Borja. This time, armed with my metal detector, I intended to go over the area thoroughly with an eye toward finding the treasure. It was late June, but "El Norte", the north wind, familiar to all who have traveled the Baja, blew cool air, and the summer heat had not yet taken over. It was one of those times when I just felt good to be out by myself, and wasn't really going to be too disappointed if I didn't find much gold, but rather just looked forward to the search itself. The days were warm, but not sweltering, and the nights were cool enough to sleep well. The food tasted good in the fresh clear air of the Sierra Assemblea, high above the desert floor, and I looked forward each day to my campfire. That time after supper when I would sit by the fire, sipping my Tequila, staring into the coals, and thinking, and dreaming, and being in such a peaceful place, was very precious to me. It was worth as much as all the gold I would find.

For almost two weeks, I worked my way through the canyons and foothills north and west of Yubay, running my metal detector over every patch of flat ground I found. There were a few promising samples of ore to be collected, but no treasure. One day I saw a horse and rider approach, following the canyon floor below me. He saw me, and approached for a talk. It turned out he was from a ranch quite a way distant, and had been looking for some lost cattle. He was a very handsome man in his early thirties, and seemed very knowledgeable about the area. He dismounted and we sat on a large rock, talking for a while. He told me his name was Juan. As was my custom in such meetings, I asked him if he had ever come across any signs of the Jesuits. He said he had not, and asked how my gold prospecting was going. I showed him some samples I had, and a small vial of gold I had gotten over the last few days. He seemed very impressed, and congratulated me, but I could tell he was not motivated to look for gold himself as some others I had shown the gold to have been. Being a rancher was fine with him, he wanted no other life. He told me about his rancho. I had heard of it, but I had never visited. Almost casually, and as an afterthought, he mentioned that he had once found the bones of a burro, and some very old wood buried at the foot of an old and long dead cardon. It may have meant little to him, but it was music to my ears! I questioned him closely. Yes, the bones did seem to be very old. And yes, the wood was the same very hard wood I described to him. I was very excited about his discovery, and determined to see it for myself. It might be nothing, I realized. Dead burros were not unusual in the desert. Yet, there were just too many similarities between his description and what

I had found years before at Desengano. He gave me very explicit directions to his rancho, and said he would be returning there the next day. He would be glad to show me the place. I told him I would meet him there. Juan asked me to be on the lookout for his lost cows, and continued down the canyon and out of sight.

That night at the campfire I pondered what I had learned that day. The part of the desert his ranch was situated on was a long way from the path I had predicted the party from San Borja would have taken. It was too far west. I sat, and thought, and slowly a new scenario began to take place in my mind. I imagined the men and mules, becoming more and more desperate to hide the relics, had wanted more distance between them and the mission at San Borja. If they had not stopped at Yubay, it is possible their water was getting low. Another burro lost as well. That would have been a real problem. I could see them discussing their deteriorating situation, and deciding to abandon their plan to continue north, but instead to turn west, and head for the Pacific coast. They might well have passed through the visita at Punta Prieta. With luck it would have been unoccupied at that time, save for some Indians, whom they did not fear. From there, with a fresh water supply, and perhaps more burros, they could have continued on to the coast. There was water available at Cordonices near Punta El Diablo. There they could make their way north on the Pacific shore, or perhaps gain passage on a ship that might happen by. The idea seemed plausible to me the more I mulled it over. I went to sleep that night filled with anticipation.

The next morning I broke camp, packed everything into my truck and followed Juan's directions to the ranch. He had ridden a long way, but his directions were good, and I drove up to the ranch around noon. I met Juan's father, who welcomed me into the house. As was the custom, the women stayed out of sight in the kitchen, but I could see them from time to time peeking in at me, and hear their hushed whispering and an occasional giggle. They did not get many visitors, much less a gringo to boot. Juan arrived just before nightfall. He had spotted his lost cows, but they had been heading back toward the ranch, so he had decided to go back for them the next day if they didn't arrive on their own. I stayed for dinner that night, and breakfast the next morning. I gave Juan and his father a box of .22 long rifle shells, and a spare five gallon can of gasoline to use in their generator. Juan went with me in my truck, pointing out the way. We could drive all but the last few hundred yards. He showed me the spot. It was much like the other one I had found, except the weathered bones were clearly visible sticking up out of the sand. We took some shovels from the truck and Juan helped me dig out the bones. Along with the bones we found a metal axle with rotted wooden spokes still partially attached. I saw immediately that the axle was from the era of the Jesuits. We were looking at objects that had been hidden almost two hundred years before. After the pit had been thoroughly excavated, with no further significant finds, I began going over the area with my metal detector. Juan had never seen such a device before, and was fascinated by it. I showed him how to use it, and he was delighted when he got a signal, and we unearthed a good sized iron nail. It was also from the Jesuits. Nothing else showed up, however, and at dusk I took Juan back to the ranch. He offered to put me up for another night, but I was anxious to get back to the site, and declined his invitation. I drove back out to the pit, and set up camp for the night.

After an early breakfast, I began searching the area again with the metal detector. I set up a search pattern, and looked in ever widening circles with the pit at the center. I worked all morning and found nothing. As was my habit, I had a light lunch of tortillas and fruit, and enjoyed a short siesta around noon. After the nap, I began sweeping the area again. I selected a little spot on a ridge, between some huge granite boulders. As I turned the machine on, it screeched loudly. I immediately turned it off and removed the headset to check the settings on the volume. They were normal. I was a bit confused, turned the detector back on and took another sweep. Again, the same loud screech. I was getting pretty excited by now. Whatever was down there was pretty dense, and pretty close to the surface. I swept the area closely to try to get a feeling for the extent of the signal. I determined that it was about two and a half feet across. I began scooping out the sand and pebbles with my hands. About nine inches down, my fingers came across a layer of the same ancient very hard wood I had found in Desengano. Just below the wood was disintegrated leather. I just sat back and stared at the leather. I knew that in the next few moments, my lifetime quest would either be gratified with success, or once again I would have a disheartening failure. With trembling hands, I continued my digging by hand, carefully scraping away the sand and pebbles.

Now, at this point, dear reader, I am going to have to ask your kind indulgence. As I am sure you will understand, and as I have pointed out previously, finding gold, or any sort of treasure, can have very serious consequences. Do you remember John Steinbeck's story entitled "The Pearl"? Lives can be ruined by good luck. If there is anyone from the Mexican Governmental Department of Antiquities reading this, I categorically deny that I found anything of value. For all other readers, work with me on this, ok?

When I returned to Bahia de los Angeles, I immediately made some calls to determine what part of antiquities a person finds belong to him. I was just curious, that's all. I was not surprised to hear that the government of Mexico would get 85%, and the finder would get 15%. That didn't seem like much compensation for years of work, determination, planning, and just plain good luck.

Returning to Las Vegas to do some more research on the subject, I found out some interesting things about valuable objects of art. At that time in Spain, if a specimen had not been reported stolen, and could be confirmed as genuine by licensed appraisers, it was entirely legal to be privately owned. I also found that normally these valuable objects were not held long by the owner. These people were often very wealthy, and the normal thing to do with such a piece of art was to inflate its value greatly, donate it to a museum, and take a large tax write-off for such generosity.

I was glad to know that in this way, many of the holy relics could be returned to their country of origin, and be viewed and enjoyed by everyone. It was a perfect end to their long journey, and to my quest to solve the mystery of their fate.

The End of an Era

As this book goes to press, I am well into my eighties, and have had to slow down a bit. I can't do all the things I used to do. Nobody my age can. I thank God I was a young man when I was. I helped my country fight and win a pretty big war, maybe the last one that was really necessary. I found the Baja waiting for me, with all its wonders, dangers, and secrets. I experienced its wonders, survived its dangers, and solved at least some of its secrets, and of that I am very proud. My mind and my heart are still in good shape, and I sometimes think about what it would be like starting all over again in this day and age. It is really so different now, I don't think I would be able to live the same wonderful life that I did.

This is the age of the big mining companies. The lone miner is pretty well relegated to the weekend hobbyist, going out to see what he can find by luck. It is not a life to him, as it was to me, but a hobby, a lark, something to do in his spare time. Serious mining of gold today is done in huge open pit mines, usually where gold is only a secondary metal. It requires a lot of capital, manpower, equipment, and permits. That is not my world, and I would never have wanted it to be. My only boss was the desert (and maybe a wife or two along the way, but briefly), and I liked it that way.

There are some things that came along in time to make my job easier. I was sure glad when I was able to put a gasoline engine on my dry washer for instance. I fought the Japanese during World War II, but I am sure glad that their country survived and was able to make transistor radios. My nights would have been a lot lonelier without one. Very recently GPS devices have changed things in the desert radically. I can now easily relocate any spot I have been if I have put in the coordinates. These things were made possible by the satellites that crisscross overhead at night. For forty years now I have been able to see them from my campfire, just after dark, or just before dawn. They can be fitted with all sorts of filters and cameras to scan wide areas of the desert for mineral deposits. Magnetic anomaly detectors can pinpoint metal masses from hundreds of miles above the earth. Every inch of the Baja has been mapped without the need to set foot on the ground.

I have no argument with all these things, they make life easier, and I have adopted many of them. But, like it or not, they do change things. Geologists come to the Baja now in helicopters. They can land in places in just minutes that took me days to reach. Using satellite communications they can talk to New York, London, or Timbuktu from the entrance of a mine in the middle of a desert. Giant jet planes cross the Baja in the stratosphere, spewing contrails, and making the clouds smell of jet fuel. I could be dying of thirst on the desert floor, while thirty thousand feet above me a businessman from Manzanillo is just starting in on his third martini.

I put no value judgment on this. It is what it is, and not me, or you, nor anyone else can roll the clock back to an earlier day. The genie is out of the bottle, and out he will stay. I look back on my life as a prospector in the Baja, and I now realize that while I lacked some of the tools that modern desert dwellers have, I also had some opportunities that they do not have, and never will, because they are gone forever. There was a sort of innocence, and openness about the Baja. The main obstacle to overcome was not the red tape of rules and regulations, nor the need for tons of equipment and supplies as it is today. Our main obstacle to overcome was nature itself – the burning desert sun, the isolation, the lack of civilization. I will take those obstacles any day over the ones that have replaced them.

I leave the desert knowing that there is a lot more gold out there. I also know that when and if it is wrested from the sands, it will be by giant machines, new methods of refining, and crews in the hundreds.

It will not be by a lone miner with a rock hammer, a dry washer, and the accumulated knowledge of how to find gold.

I will stack my lifetime of experiences and memories up against those of any other man. I have made a lot of money, probably more than most men. I have spent it all, some well, on helping friends and family, cases of good Mexican beer, and trips to Las Vegas where I used the money to its maximum value. Oh, of course, I blew a little on alimony, insurance, gasoline, taxes and other wasteful pursuits, but not much.

When I die, I will probably be buried with my rock hammer in my hand. And I will still have it when I meet St. Peter at the pearly gates. I will be surprised to be there, figuring that some of my past indiscretions would indicate another form of eternal residence below. Saint Peter will see the rock hammer in my hand, and tell me

"Oh, no, not another miner! I can't let another miner in here!"

"Why not?" I ask.

"Why all these miners are tearing the place up," he says, "they are ripping up the golden streets, melting down the golden harps, and just causing a mess."

I think a minute, then say to St. Peter, "Tell you what, I will make you a deal. If you let me in, I will get rid of them all for you. Deal?"

"Ok, but you have only one day. Come on in."

The next day, I am lying back on a soft cloudbank, enjoying the harp music, when St. Peter comes along.

"They are all gone! Great! How did you do that, Herman?"

"Simple," says I, "I just told them there was a new big gold strike in Hell!"

It's an old joke, but it does have a grain of truth in it. Miners live for that next find, the mother lode. It is in their blood – and mine.

About the Author

$\mathcal{R}$oger Silliman has made his home in the little paradise of Bahia de los Angeles since 2002, having traveled there on vacations many times over a period of thirty years. Dr. Silliman earned a Ph.D. from the University of Southern California, spending many years as a Professor of Instructional Technology, and later as a college administrator, and business owner in California.

The "As Told To" author is deeply indebted to Herman Hill for being allowed to share these stories.

Printed in the United States
129107LV00002B/125/P